Escape Your Illusions

VIVEK ACHARY

ISBN: 151931325X
ISBN-13: 978-1519313256

To people everywhere
often derogatorily referred to
as 'consumers'

CONTENTS

Acknowledgments   i

Introduction   1

1   Illusions Are Invisible   7

Reality Check #1   16

2   What Illusions Do To Us   18

3   What Illusions Do To Our World   25

Reality Check #2   29

4   How Illusions Survive   30

5   Illusions About Alcohol   38

Reality Check #3   47

6   Illusions About War   49

7   Illusions About Smoking   56

8   Illusions About Religion   60

9   Illusions About Profits   67

10	Illusions About Time	72
11	Illusions About Food	80
	Reality Check #4	86
12	Illusions About Water	87
13	Illusions About Pollution	91
14	Illusions About Product Innovation	95
15	Illusions About Career	100
16	Illusions About Education	105
17	Illusions About Gender Equality	111
18	Illusions About Health	117
19	Illusions About Appearances	126
20	Illusions About Attention Spans	130
21	Illusions About Work-Life Balance	133
22	Illusions About Culture	136
23	Why Escape Your Illusions?	140
	Bibliography	143

ACKNOWLEDGMENTS

Thanks to the editorial team and everyone at Create Space for making this book possible.

I am grateful to my dear friends and colleagues who took the time to review the manuscript and provide their valuable comments: Viresh for his logical arguments and detailed thoughts; Bhalekar for adding a touch of positivity; Saba for his marketing savvy and compelling business storytelling that rubbed off on me, eventually; and Prakash for sharing his practical wisdom.

Also, thanks to all those who have provided their encouragement and support: Sayed Sarwar Ali who has been a family friend, mentor, and guide; and the IIT-B batch of 1990 especially Anu, Sanjay, TK, Wanage, Wilfred, Alluri, Surya, Shashi, Senthil, and the rest of the gang. Thanks to Suhas, Seebah, VD, and Santosa for sharing their amazing stories, and Bhatta for setting me off on this journey all those years ago.

What I owe my family really can't be put into words: I'm deeply grateful to my parents for, above all, introducing me to the world of books; my sister and brother for their unconditional support; and my wife and son for making me believe, and putting up with my numerous foibles.

maya (mä-yə), noun: A subtle force that creates the grand illusion that the world that we see is real

INTRODUCTION

"And a lovely revolution to you too, sir."

On 25 January 2011, a young economics consultant in Cairo, known only as TravellerW, pulled out his mobile phone at 11.42 am and tweeted out those words.

Tension had been brewing for days in Egypt, with vast sections of the population fed up with the country's leadership.

Some minutes later there was a reply, "Internet's back in #Egypt." Shortly after came another reply, and another, and another.

A couple of hours later the tweets began to get ominous, "This will get ugly quick," Sandmonkey tweeted.

And get ugly it did.

Security forces disguised as civilians were joined by thugs and penetrated the pro-change demonstrators who had taken to the streets. They led a charge on horses and camels, whipping the crowds as they rode through.

Rocks were thrown at them. They retaliated with guns and tanks.

The pro-change demonstrators suffered terrible losses. But they refused to budge. By the next day, they had pushed back the tyrannical security forces and taken over the city.

Soon the dictatorship fell.

It all started with those few words, typed into a mobile screen, which snowballed into a deluge of tweets as thousands of people poured into the streets, capturing the imagination of millions around the world—no mean feat in this age of allegedly declining attention spans—and started a revolution that resulted in the toppling of the ruling government in Egypt.

It has often been showcased as the ultimate testimony to the power of digital communications.

Soon afterwards, in a different part of the world, a girl named Malala Yousafzai, all of 13 years old at the time, had a burning wish for something many of us take for granted—she wanted to go to school.

Just for having this desire, Malala was shot in the head. It was an assassination attempt by the Taliban while she was in a school bus in the Swat district of northwestern Pakistan.

They failed. She survived.

A year later, in 2013, armed with a smart phone and zero marketing budget, she achieved the reach and power that media corporations would have given an arm and a leg for, a few decades ago.

While digital communications have made reaching out to millions of the proverbial target audience cheaper and easier than ever before, world-changing messages like those by TravellerW and Malala are, by far, the exception.

The paradox is that though there are literally hundreds and thousands of communication channels today to connect with, well, whoever you want, making a *real* connection with one's intended—and sometimes unsuspecting—audience has become even more elusive, not easier than before.

So, what's going on?

The pre-digital era had an inbuilt system of checks and balances.

Editors and proof readers screened content before they were published.

Film rolls, the development of negatives, and printing of photographs each had a cost, so photographers were a bit more particular about what they shot.

Books are a lot harder to delete than blog posts.

What digitization has achieved is to remove the screening of content, opening the floodgates of self expression to everyone in the e-world who wants their voice to be heard. In principle, this has been 'A Good Thing', and voices such as those of TravelerW and Malala have changed the world for the better.

They are, however, not the only voices.

If a person was exposed to hundreds of messages in the pre-digital era, today she has a million or more to deal with. Most of them are unscreened, un-reviewed, and unedited.

This has led to a fundamental fuzziness of thinking that—while existent earlier—has grown more pronounced. Simplicity has been replaced by complexity. Factual authority has been swamped by a diversity of opinions and sometimes resulted in multiple versions of the truth. Like the evanescence of a blog post or website that is here today and gone tomorrow, our beliefs and value systems are also in a state of flux.

This is, at once, a huge problem and a glorious opportunity.

The only thing that can prevent digital communications from exacerbating the problems that existed in the pre-digital era, and help us ride the waves of change that it offers is the clarity of our own thoughts.

Unfortunately, our thoughts are the primary target of most, if not all, communications.

Every message is aimed at swaying, influencing, bending, cajoling, coaxing, and sometimes, downright intimidating us into one or the other way of thinking.

Our personas are, to a large extent, the product of our conditioning, which in turn is driven by the messages drilled into us in different forms.

We *are* the messages we get.

When these messages diverge—deliberately or unwittingly—from the essence of reality that governs all life on the planet and in the universe, it leads to a state of delusion where we strongly believe, uphold, fight, and sometimes die for ideas that are fundamentally unreal.

This delusional state of being has been referred to in ancient times, long before digital communications came into the picture, as *maya*—an illusion about what reality really is. This state can exist at many levels and impacts our lives in many ways. It can function at a superficial, material level, that results in parting us from our money. At its deepest level, it concerns the very 'fabric of reality' of the world we live in.

We can find illusions in everything, from the material world of stuff sold in supermarkets, to scientific studies about the nature of matter—the supposedly 'solid' things that make up life, the universe, and everything.

Escaping from this state calls for a continuous and conscious awareness that dispels the illusions at every level as we encounter them.

The very first step to escape from illusions is to fine-tune our awareness of external factors that influence our perception of reality, so that we may be free from oppressive, regressive, restrictive, or simply unnecessary ideas and notions, and ultimately regain control of the most precious gift we all have been given—our finite time on this earth.

Most of the digital communications we encounter has multiplied, complicated, and intensified the illusions around us. That's mostly what this book is about.

The next step to real freedom from illusions is the conscious cultivation of deeper levels of awareness of reality—beyond the stuff that is taught in quantum physics courses at educational institutions. It is the awareness gained from the ugliness and despair as well as the beauty and bliss of our personal experiences. This route has been termed *neti neti*—a Sanskrit term literally meaning 'not this, not this'—or *via negativa* in Latin.

It is an approach to life where we go through one experience after another, stumbling, falling, and picking ourselves up, and by trial and error, finally experience the essence of pure reality.

Poets and mystics call it an inner journey.

It is, however, pointless to discuss the illusion of *matter*, in a world that has not even got over the illusion of the *material*. As an old pop song went, "We're living in a material world…"

The point of this book is that this materialism—the unending desire for 'things'—is essentially alien to human nature. It is an artificial notion that is planted in the minds of people, deliberately or otherwise. Even so, this kind of illusion really would not have been a problem if it wasn't for the disastrous effects it has on the quality of human life and the planet.

Getting rid of many of the superficial illusions that have hijacked our precious time is an important first step of our own inner journeys, where we experience the absolute, magical wonder, the sheer cosmic majesty of reality *as it really is*, and not as we have been led to believe it is, for way too long.

The ideas presented in this book, hopefully, will create the awareness that takes us to the starting point of our own inner journeys.

1 ILLUSIONS ARE INVISIBLE

One morning, at a border checkpoint between two countries, a young man in uniform sharply clicked his heels, saluting smartly as he reported for his first day at work as a border security guard.

He was instructed to keep an eye on everyone who crossed the border. Taking his job very seriously, he proceeded to inspect every man, woman, and beast that stepped over his line.

In the evening, an old man rode by lazily, crossing the border with a huge, suspicious-looking package on his bicycle.

Naturally the guard proceeded to stop and make him empty the whole package, turn every article it contained upside down and inside out. Hours later, it was almost dark.

He had found nothing.

Reluctantly he allowed the old man to leave and he shuffled away, for his papers seemed very much in order.

The next day, to his bafflement, he saw the old man again, coming from the same direction as the evening before, riding in without a care—and with yet another suspicious-looking bag on his cycle.

The story repeated itself, and the guard had to let the old man off.

To make a rather long story short, the same events occurred almost every single day of the young guard's career, until one fine day, he was due to retire.

Like clockwork, the old man, who was impervious to age it seems, rode in over the horizon. The guard stopped him and said, "Look, old man, I *know* you've been up to something fishy all along. Today is my last day at work. Just tell me what you've been doing and I'll let you go free."

Smiling toothlessly, the old man replied, "Smuggling bicycles."

THE BLIND SPOT OF HUMANITY

Sometimes it is hard to focus on what is right before our eyes. We are like the guard who couldn't see the bicycles for what they were, all through his life. That is the nature of illusions.

They are all around us, day in and day out, as we swim through life. Yet most of us fail to see them. We are like the young fish that asked its mother, "What is water?"

The problem is not that these illusions are manufactured, deep inside some secret underground facility or soundproof boardroom, as part of a conspiracy against the human race.

The problem is that they are right out there in the open, everywhere you look, hiding in plain sight.

Yet, we all like to think we are a bunch of realists. We know what's real and what's illusory, right?

By the time a human being is eighteen, she or he has been exposed to about a million marketing messages. We know these messages sell products, services, causes, presidents, deals, news, alerts, and so on. In fact, most of us have developed filters for these messages that intrude into our daily consciousness, more often than not, uninvited and unwelcome. Thus, we assume, we are inured to their effects.

The question is: how effective are our filters in immunizing us?

Do they *really* offer 100% protection?

Do we have any study about the short- and long-term effects that millions of messages have on that massive information-soaking sponge called the human brain?

Are they helping us to be more 'successful'?

Or do they bring us any closer to the all-time-favorite human goal of 'happiness'?

Happiness, by the way, is a strange thing. One doesn't need to ask children below about five years if they are happy because the answer is usually writ large on their faces—unless of course, some adult messed up, and maybe forgot to feed them or change their diapers or something like that.

Children don't know what unhappiness is. For that matter, *they don't know what happiness is either.*

They simply *are* happy, due to their capacity for *eidetic perception*, which makes them as fascinated by coffee cups as Jumbo jets, by cardboard boxes as much as giant shape-changing robots.

In that sense, perhaps the only place true democracy exists is in the minds of children. To them, all things truly are equal.

We are all born into this state of bliss and yet, somehow, almost all of us manage to lose it along the way.

Eidetic perception is a fascinating ability that helps us see things as they are—miracles. Show a coffee cup or cardboard box to adults, it will instantaneously trigger a neuron in our brains that causes us to simply ignore it. The problem is that we *know* everything there is to know about coffee cups and cardboard boxes too well. We *know* that coffee cups and cardboard boxes merely carry something useful temporarily and, once that coffee or parcel is consumed, are useless empty containers that need to be discarded.

The child's democratic brain has been replaced by a value-seeking brain, which is driven by a whole lot of aspirations, expectations, and priorities; coffee cups and cardboard boxes don't figure very high on the list. They are pretty much at the bottom of our internal value hierarchy, probably ranked just above garbage, and hence we would consider ourselves very foolish if we paid much attention to them.

We adults unconsciously place a value on every single thing, which determines our corresponding responses to those things.

Pre-school children—kids whose minds have not yet been messed up by adults through the process ironically called 'education'—on the other hand, find coffee cups and cardboard boxes absolutely fascinating. On a comparative scale, it would equal an adult's fascination with, say, a red Ferrari or the *Koh-i-noor* diamond. Try snatching away a child's cardboard box and see what happens, if you already haven't experienced this.

Parents often get frustrated when they give really cool electronic toys to children, only to find them totally neglecting the toy, while all their attention is devoted to the cardboard boxes they came in. That's because electronic gadgets only rank highly on the adult's value system, not the child's. By ascribing value to everything, we systematically and progressively—or regressively, rather—make life unhappy for ourselves.

The remedy, of course, is not to abandon value systems nor to go back to playing with cardboard boxes and coffee cups, it is to regain the *ability to see eidetically*. It is our only chance for stable and enduring happiness. We all experience happiness in short bursts: when a significant other says, "Yes," or when we find a job or pot of gold, or scale a mountain or become a parent. These bursts of happiness are often notoriously short-lived, and not at the same level that we experience as children. In fact, the only reason we hope and search for sources of happiness is that we were happy to begin with.

Indeed, we would all have given up the search a long time ago but for the fact that we have had a glimpse of bliss, and loved it. While few of us remember our early childhood, most of it remains perfectly preserved in unconscious memories that direct the course of our lives.

As we grow into adults, this childhood bliss slowly fades away from our awareness, as our conscious minds find more 'important' things to do. The void created by this slow and unnoticed loss of bliss gets replaced by an inexplicable longing—for *something*.

Our typical response to this niggling, restless emptiness is to fill it with activity. So we usually address this longing through diversions: an exam, a degree, a job, a career, a game, a goal, a girl, a guy, a child, a vacation, an adventure, a God, an experience, *something* to fill the void.

While all these are diversions, many of us fall for the illusion that they are the main focus of our lives. And though all these pursuits bring their own rewards, nothing ever quite matches up to the pure joy we once knew, which is what we really seek.

Does it have to be that way?

Everybody already seems to have the answer to this question but here it is anyway—what causes us to lose the bliss that we knew as children?

It's often dismissively attributed to a process called 'growing up', but why should the mere act of growing up cause unhappiness? It is something every single child looks forward to, until they actually do.

Then there is the argument that 'ignorance is bliss' and children are ignorant.

Does knowledge make us unhappy?

If so, all the Ph.Ds of the world would be the unhappiest people around, yet there is no correlation between one's level of knowledge and happiness.

The majority would concur that adulthood brings responsibilities that children don't have. *Quod erat demonstrandum.*

Do responsibilities cause discontent?

On the contrary, the greatest responsibilities, such as raising a family or pursuing a dream, are immensely fulfilling. Probably, issues begin to arise when those responsibilities involve setting up and striving for progressively steeper goals.

If we fail, we are miserable and stressed out.

If we succeed we have a temporary respite—when we get that promotion, or baby, or villa, or million dollars, or complete our child's education, or get them married, or something—until the next goal comes up.

Retirement.

Nest eggs.

World tours.

World peace.

Landing on Mars.

Whatever.

So the problem neither has anything to do with 'growing up', nor gaining knowledge, nor having to face responsibilities. It is because there is no end in sight. Each step takes us tantalizingly closer, but *that* bliss is always just round the corner, after the next step, just out of reach. Growing up essentially involves stepping onto an infinite treadmill, and the illusion we all have is that *we are on it by choice.*

Why do we set these goals for ourselves?

Why do we lose our child-like bliss and trade it in for the lives most of us lead as adults?

What about those millions of messages that we are bombarded with every day of our lives? Could it be that those messages, usually uninvited and often unwelcome, have something to do with our loss of bliss?

This bombardment of messages was long ago labeled as 'information overload' and neatly tucked away in our collective minds, out of sight.

We have unconsciously fallen into a habit of labeling things, as if that somehow explains anything or makes them more manageable.

We can talk about gravity and chlorophyll and quarks and bosons and dark matter but this knowledge is limited and, sooner or later, we all come up against a wall of ignorance beyond which we are clueless.

For instance, ask someone why 'gravity' exists and, if they have some knowledge about physics, they would reply that it's because of something called 'mass'. Essentially, what we are doing is explaining the *label* called gravity with *another label* called mass. Go a step further and ask why mass exists? One is pretty certain to draw a blank.

It's the same with every single subject in the universe.

Clearly, the process of labeling things is not quite the same as knowing things and definitely does nothing towards solving a problem.

Labeling the messages that we receive every day of our lives as 'information overload' does not make the issue go away. In fact, it doesn't go anywhere. One by one, day by day, those messages take up residence in our brains and strongly, silently, and permanently dictate the life choices we make.

The presence of messages is so all-pervasive and ubiquitous that every single thought *that we think is our own* fundamentally stems from some sort of external conditioning.

Everything in our lives, from the choice of our clothes and mates, our children's schools and colleges, our lifestyles, our career choices, our family lives, our achievements, who we love, what we hate, what cars we drive, who we vote for, what we eat and drink, right up to what coffin we choose when we finally exit the stage of life is determined by one thing alone—the messages we carry around in our brains.

Many of these messages, and consequently our beliefs and illusions, are created by marketing, that irresistible and utterly superficial world that is packaged and sold to us by every screaming billboard. Every TV spot. Every marketing message that we have ever seen.

What this has 'achieved' is to basically take a miracle called life and transform it into a grotesque, walking-talking-eating-sleeping billboard of product endorsements and marketing-fueled ideologies and opinions.

Naturally, this makes those among us who are conscious of the overt and covert bombardment of marketing messages tend to consider advertisers and marketers as the bad guys.

Yet, it is not marketers alone who are to blame.

Every movie that we see, every news item that we read, every idol we adore, every admiring or disapproving glance of our neighbors, every whispered comment by society, and now, every social media message that is shared with us is a marketing message in disguise.

The term marketing is actually much wider in scope than a mere corporate function. Everyone we interact with is involved in some form of marketing. We sell them our ideas. They sell us theirs. Few personal and professional relationships and social interactions are free of the colors of an underlying marketing message.

Unless, of course, you are a child.

One of the biggest illusions we all have is the illusion of being in control. We like to think that we have it all covered, most of the time at least. That we are somehow exempt from the illusion, either because we are smarter, or think more deeply, or are simply immune to it.

Are we really?

We can find out right now by taking a simple and rather pleasant test.

REALITY CHECK #1

Go on a vacation for as long as possible.

It doesn't matter if we are along or with our family or just friends. The only caveat is that, during the entire vacation, we consciously cut off all exposure to media and work-related communication.

No phone calls.

No email.

No TV.

No movies.

No newspapers.

And definitely no Facebook—or any other social media.

This may seem impossible, but actually it is not.

Ideally a two-week vacation works best, but if that's not possible, one needs to do this for two–three days at the very least. (Incidentally, a much more demanding form of 'vacation' is the *vipassana* meditation program, where not only exposure to media, but diets, schedules, and even conversations are controlled.)

The next thing to do, as we get back from our vacation, is to carefully observe the changes within us as we re-expose ourselves to media, news, and work.

Not superficial changes such as the weather or the absence of sunny beaches, obviously, but subtle, internal changes within ourselves—pulse rate, stress level, emotions, and reactions to situations.

If we do this right, we will even be able to notice the changes caused by such ostensibly harmless things such as, for instance, fluorescent lighting.

And if we notice that our internal system changes—and almost certainly it will—then unfortunately, it means that our notion of being in control is an illusion.

Even our pulse rate is determined by external factors.

A young executive once approached his boss for the approval of his leave application. His company package offered a three-week annual leave, on paper at least, and all that the poor chap wanted was two weeks off.

He thought he had earned it but what he was told was, "Everyone here is overloaded, and markets are tough. So if our department can continue to function without you for two weeks, then probably we don't need you at all."

He curtailed his vacation.

Most of us have been there.

So this test may be difficult but we owe it to ourselves and—believe it or not—all of humankind. Two questions that it is important to ask are:

1.   What have our illusions done to us internally?

2.   What have our illusions done to everything around us—our environment and society?

2 WHAT ILLUSIONS DO TO US

At trade shows and product exhibitions in the Middle East, Africa, and the Indian subcontinent, the weather outside the sometimes air-conditioned halls is either hot—or hotter. The mercury hovers around 100°F, give or take a few degrees. The heat is killing.

Yet you will find the majority of participants dressed in western formals: suits, ties, and all.

The reason people dress that way is the illusion that somehow, it makes them look more 'professional'. Yet if they were to dress according to what the weather dictated, they would follow the traditional attire of their regions: loose-fitting, flowing robes designed after centuries of practical experience.

Has there been any fashion or marketing bible that stipulated their 'chosen' attire? No.

And yet that is the message that is so deeply embedded in their psyche that they are willing to sweat for days to abide by it.

While the attire at exhibitions is an extreme example, these misconceptions extend to daily wear too. In many countries, their traditional clothes, which are best suited to their climates, are simply not available in stores.

That is just one of almost countless examples of how messages enter our brain and direct our life, usually uninvited and often unwelcome.

In Asian rock bands, especially in the 1990s when globalization and the arrival of satellite TV made it possible for them to reach audiences worldwide for the first time, an overwhelming majority of the groups' members tended to wear dark sunglasses.

Of course, many rock band members the world over tend to wear shades—either to look cool or hide the previous night's hangover. But the inordinate number of Asian bands favoring shades seemed to suggest that this had little to do with bright sunshine or bleary eyes.

Did it have something to do with disguising their country of origin, that the typical shape of their eyes would instantly give away, the rationale being that this would increase the 'acceptability' of their music?

Again, has it ever been written that Asians would be debarred from music for having narrow eyes? Certainly not.

Yet, if a survey had actually been conducted *and* the band members were aware of their own complexes *and* had they answered candidly, that is precisely what it may have shown.

In fact, a different kind of study *has* been conducted to identify the most popular type of cosmetic surgery in Asian countries. Not surprisingly, it's eyelid surgery—the east Asian blepharoplasty, a procedure through which people of Mongoloid descent with a single eyelid can get a crease to make it a double eyelid. In South Korea, women get eye surgeries as wedding gifts.

What many cultures and races suffer from is a deep psychological trauma inflicted by others—and themselves—over centuries, about their physical traits.

Many dark-skinned races, such as Asian Indians, have an obsession with 'fair skin'.

Illusions about fairness are so out of hand that recently in Ghana, the government banned all fairness creams totally. In India, where public opinion was against the derogatory representation of dark skinned people—such as advertisements portraying them being rejected at job interviews and as marriage partners—marketers worked around legal issues by labeling fairness creams as 'blemish removal creams'.

How can people be happy when there is such fundamental discontent inside them? They literally are miserable living in their own skin.

The converse is also true, epitomized in the phrase, 'the white man's burden', which needs little elaboration.

Whether positive or negative, such biases have no basis in reality—not the *real* reality anyway—and have everything to do with false perceptions.

HOW ILLUSIONS CHANGE US

The short answer: almost completely.

There is not a single aspect of our life that is not a direct or indirect product of messages. The glaring irony is that we like to think of ourselves as 'self made'—even the son of a U.S. president was allegedly offended when someone suggested otherwise.

These messages that we carry in our brains—our inner illusions—form the nucleus of our very being, like the seed of a tree. When we examine our lives—*if* we examine our lives at all—we only tend to look at the branches and leaves and fruits.

Naturally such efforts are doomed to fail.

ESCAPE YOUR ILLUSIONS

What we really ought to take a look at is the core of our unconscious thoughts that drive us to do the things we do.

That is the insidiousness of messages. And the perpetrators are spread far, far beyond the creators of mere advertisements.

Maybe you still think you haven't been bitten by the *maya* bug.

Or maybe, you came up against your illusions, gave them a label, and forgot about them.

Along with being in control, the thought of being self-made ranks among our favorite illusions that our minds are unlikely to readily give up.

Yet giving up those illusions is the most essential part of escaping the world of *maya*, if we are to regain true control over our decisions and live our lives on our own terms.

Why bother?

For starters, our illusions are *expensive*. They make us buy things.

Secondly, that money has to be earned.

This in turn makes us remain on the treadmill much, much longer than necessary.

This, finally, leaves us little time to do the things that really matter.

The aim of this book is not to make people renounce the material world. There is nothing wrong with material things *per se*. Matter is not evil. The aim is to get rid of illusions and self-defeating, false beliefs.

In the so-called 'normal' course of life, escaping one's illusions is a lot easier said than done.

Actually, it is next to impossible.

The proliferation of escape routes—by taking spiritual courses, going on adventure holidays, taking vacations, traveling around the world, and through other distractions—would suggest that most everywhere in the world, people need getaways.

What exactly are we all getting away from? Our daily lives?

Why not lead lives that don't require this periodic getting-away-from in the first place?

Many people have spoken volumes about this, in many different words.

Carlos Castaneda in *The Journey to Ixtlan* [1] called it 'stopping the world'. Unfortunately, his journey was fueled by *peyote* or mescaline, a psychotropic drug. Some prescribe expanding the mind through cannabis.

The problem is that this expansion is a temporary feeling, and mostly only complicates the illusions that we are trying to get rid of, which are largely responsible for creating a state of mind that needs drugs to calm it down in the first place.

Do children need external aids to find their bliss? So why should adults? And, what if the pusher is out of stock? There is much outcry to legalize marijuana in many countries. Actually the question whether or not it should be legal is irrelevant. The widespread tendency to smoke pot or consume other drugs does not reflect how wonderful drugs are, but rather how miserable our lives are. The state of bliss associated with drugs ought to be our *normal state* of being. Our body can manufacture enough dopamine and melatonin to make us feel high without any external help. What have we done to our natural bliss?

Some writers have called the process of escaping our

illusions as *ba-mahk*, or 'feeling the pulse' of the universe.

Mystics routinely advise us to 'find our center'.

The mystic, Ramakrishna Paramahamsa, the spiritual teacher of the more famous Swami Vivekananda, described the experience of raising our awareness as 'an elephant entering a small hut'.

Some suggest chanting hymns as the path to awareness. While sound vibrations *are* powerful, they need to be done in *a certain way*, which few actually can. Done incorrectly, chanting has the real danger of putting one to sleep—physically and metaphorically.

Then there is the global favorite: meditation, which however, is usually equated with some sort of cosmic lullaby. It is not. It is an explosive process of awakening one's inner energies. The calm that is associated with meditation is a *result* of the release and smoother flow of energy within one's system. To approach meditation as 'a process that calms the senses' truly is to put the cart before the horse.

All these tools and descriptions, even those coming from the most well-meaning of souls, unfortunately, don't take us any closer to our goal any more than a signboard takes us to our destination.

Probably, the most accurate description about losing our illusions can be found in the ancient Hindu text, the *Bhagavad Gita*, where the process is described as 'shooting the eye of a bird by looking its reflection in a pond'.

Many misconstrue this as a description of the skill of the archer—a rather bland and unimaginative interpretation. It actually poetically explains the real complexity of keeping track of our sensory perceptions, our own mind, the factory of discontent-producing illusions in human lives.

If we actually try it, we find that a thought is, at risk of sounding clichéd, more slippery than an eel.

Every time we try to pin a thought down, it shifts, and like a wily foe, changes shape and hue, it moves, it throws up distractive counter thoughts, and generally does everything an eel would, to avoid being 'caught' in the net of our probing awareness.

And yet, it is possible to become so acutely aware of one's thoughts—and illusions—to the point of being able to feel the firing of a single neuron in our brain, and track down the exact feeling we had before the neuron fired, what caused it to fire, and what we feel afterwards.

With heightened levels of awareness, losing one's illusions is actually quite easy, and can happen in one Zen-like instant.

When such awareness happens, life is poetry.

Once we 'break on through to the other side', life takes on an altogether different dimension. Every moment of every day, through all the highs and lows, life is a one unshakeable, fascinating experience after another.

Awareness forms the bedrock from which we experience *the same things* at a different—and a whole lot more fulfilling—level of consciousness.

This is not about great achievements or stupendous material success, though indeed they may occur as by-products of our awareness.

This is about enjoying cardboard boxes and empty coffee cups.

Without illusions, we are like children once again.

3 WHAT ILLUSIONS DO TO OUR WORLD

There is an ancient parable still told in the villages of western India about a young man by the name of Shekh Chilli, the less-than-bright son of a farmer who was given the task of cutting a branch of a tree that had grown too long and was intruding into the window of his house.

The young man promptly climbed the offending branch, axe in hand, and began chopping away at it, attacking the part of the branch that was closer to the tree from where he sat, so it was evident that he was soon headed for a fall.

Some kind passersby pointed this out to him, but he had the confidence of the fool and paid no heed to their warnings.

Soon of course, the inevitable happened and gravity took its course.

We all take it for granted that we are way smarter than that village idiot but our actions seem to show quite the opposite.

HOW ILLUSIONS CHANGE OUR WORLD

Do a brief Google search on climate change and you'll find tons—you've probably seen it all before—of data [2] like this:

The U.S. has 5% of the world's population, but consumes more than 30% of its resources. If all countries were to go 'the American way', we would need five planets, yet the American way is what *most developing countries aspire to emulate.*

100 billion plastic bags are thrown away every year, of which 99 billion are not recycled, killing 1 billion birds and mammals through plastic ingestion.

Nearly a billion tons of carbon dioxide are emitted by cars every year and 6 million tons of garbage, mostly plastic, are dumped in the oceans—which, incidentally, *produce most of our oxygen, not trees.*

About 100 plant and animal species die every day, many of which hold the potential to cure ailments including some forms of cancer.

The U.S. spends $35 billion annually to fight obesity, while $20 billion is all that is required to feed every starving and malnourished person on earth.

Bottled water in the U.S. consumes 1.5 million barrels of oil for transportation and costs 10,000 times more than tap water. Wouldn't it be cheaper to stop contaminating natural water sources? Yes. The real question probably is: would it be more profitable?

This list could go on forever.

Either we disbelieve these statistics—after all, who's ever verified any of these numbers?—or we shrug and move on.

The sad fact is that, though we are indeed smarter than that village idiot, we feel that *there is little we can do.*

In reality though, we can do *a lot*. Because we *caused* it.

One of the main reasons we maintain the illusions that may be destroying the planet is this: we think *everybody else is doing the same*.

One terrible night, my neighbor took it upon himself to learn to play the violin. Let's just say, cats being strangled by sadists would have produced less awful sounds.

If he didn't quite succeed at mastering the instrument, it certainly wasn't for lack of trying.

Day in and day out, the fellow would plug away at it. I suspect he couldn't have told a sharp note from a flat if they climbed on his shoulder and smacked him in the face.

Finally I decided I'd had enough and knocked on his door and suggested he take up something less destructive, like gardening. At least the plants wouldn't scream when he went to work on them.

His jaw-dropping response was, "Who's stopping *you* from learning to play the violin?"

I'm currently checking the prices of soundproof walls.

The point is, we often think that something is 'okay' if everybody else is doing the same.

Most people would agree that going against a crowd takes courage. Yes, but it takes more than courage.

It takes clarity of thought.

Clarity of thought requires awareness.

Awareness takes time.

And *time* is what we all are short of, isn't it?

William Henry Davies' unforgettable line, "What is this life if full of care, we have no time to stand and stare," was as much poetry as a prophecy. Today, more than poetic musing, it is a fundamental issue on which hinges the quality of our lives, and oh yeah, the survival of many living species on the earth. Time is the most precious commodity we have in our life. We already know all that, right?

Yet, illusions convince the best among us to trade our time for things that *seem* precious but have little genuine value. As a result, instead of lives brimming with our birthright of joy and bliss, we end up with habits and behaviors that do little for our happiness, a collection of achievements and possessions that mean little in the ultimate sense, and a life that is just ho-hum.

Still not convinced that most of us lack the awareness needed to escape our illusions?

Here's another test, simpler than the first, by an Indian mystic called *Sadhguru*, and it can be done right now.

REALITY CHECK #2

Sit erect comfortably in a chair with your legs uncrossed. Close your eyes and lightly place your open palms facing upward with the fingers together, not apart, on your thighs.

Breathe slowly, a little deeper than usual, observing your breathing.

After about 15 seconds, turn your palms so that they face downward, fingers together.

If you've done it right, you should feel a subtle but very distinct change in your breathing.

If merely changing the way we place our palms changes the very way we breathe, consider all the movements, all the postures, all the activities we go through, every day, every moment of our lives.

How aware are we really about the impact of every action on our lives?

4 HOW ILLUSIONS SURVIVE

The human body is a sophisticated, ultra-sensitive machine. The way we sit, stand, walk, run, and lie down—on our sofas, easy chairs, bean bags, toilet seats, concrete pavements, jogging tracks, mattresses, and so on—throughout our days and nights makes a huge impact on our general well-being, which we are barely aware of, if at all.

Meanwhile we confidently prescribe solutions for joint aches, back aches, spinal problems, stiff necks, bad knees, and a whole bunch of troubles that plague our bodies.

We have developed an entire field of study called ergonomics, which essentially tries to fix all the posture-related ills that didn't exist in the first place—until we created them.

For instance, many of our physical ailments would simply go away if we used thinner and firmer mattresses, threw out our sofas and chairs, and returned to squatting instead of using the crapper.

Some may argue, "Yes, we are aware about how our bodies are affected by what we do, but we can't be bothered every instant. We just don't care all that much." Yet the sales of medical and accident insurance, health foods and fads, safety airbags and devices, burglar alarms and surveillance cameras, ergonomic seating and office spaces, to name a few, all tell a different story—we do care.

WHAT'S YOUR NAME, BOB?

On an underground radio channel that existed long before the Internet days, there was a spoof of an interview with a rock music legend called Bob.

In the course of the mostly one-sided talk, as Bob was stoned out of his senses, the interviewer asked him if he was ready for a 'personal' question.

Bob mumbled an affirmative reply.

The interviewer said, "Okay, here's the question." Slowly enunciating the words, he continued, "Bob. What. Is. Your. Name?"

Bob was way too high to answer, so the interviewer helpfully goes on to give him some clues.

He says, "It's a three-letter word."

No reply from Bob.

The interviewer continues generously, "It starts with a B."

Still no reply from Bob who is now desperately racking his brain.

The interviewer goes on, "It ends with a B."

Finally, after some more prodding, the interviewer finally blurts the answer, and a palpably delighted Bob choruses, a few microseconds later.

When it comes to understanding the impact our physical actions, we are no better than a bunch of Bobs.

Our senses are so unaware, deadened, to the flowing movements—or even the existence—of energy in our systems, that it is no surprise that physical ailments are part and parcel of modern life.

Beyond the physical effects, however, our mental illusions have much deeper and more devastating effects, which make it necessary to understand what causes them.

You may have noticed that much of sales and marketing jargon—the primary suspect in the creation of illusions—revolves around war.

One of the best-selling books on the subject is titled *Marketing Warfare*.

We talk about *capturing* markets.

We have a sales *force*.

We aim to *crush* the competition.

In fact, our war-mongering mentality goes way beyond marketing.

From the time we go to school, then college, and then onto our careers or businesses, we are trained to compete.

Winning is impossible without beating the competition—or so we are led to believe.

The class toppers win medals.

The star performers get promotions—well, most of the time, at least.

As a once-popular old song goes, 'The Winner Takes It All'.

Parents exhort their kids to perform and push them to achieve.

An advertisement for a racing club shows a group of male sperm cells in the womb with a headline that reminds us that we are born to race.

So, is it morally or ethically wrong, this race to win at everything? No.

The point is not to belittle our pursuit of excellence and high levels of achievement. It is to question our *motivation* for excellence and high achievement.

Competition is taught to us pretty much from the day we are born, but *the strands of our DNA seem wired for the exact opposite—collaboration.*

The neighboring countries of India and Pakistan have maintained an overt attitude of rivalry for well over half a century, even actually going to war with each other several times. Yet, once outside their fiercely guarded borders, in the UK and Canada, for instance, you will find many Indians and Pakistanis *going out of their way to help each other.*

Our collaborative streak is even more strikingly evident during natural disasters when people across nationalities, races, and religions come forward in heart-warming demonstrations of the real side of human nature.

We are taught that success involves defeating others but we truly enjoy 'our' success when it is measured by 'their' victories.

This may seem a bit difficult to understand, much less accept, especially in a marketing or nationalistic context, where it begs the obvious questions:

How can my company be more successful if my competitor captures my share of market?

How can my country be more successful when my neighbor—or indeed some country halfway across the globe—is busy bombing our cities?

Going a step further, why do companies compete at all? Why do nations go to war in the first place?

Hatred is *something we learn* from history books and the speeches of politicians.

Love, on the other hand, is *what we are made of.*

Our lives and loves, businesses and careers, education and emancipation are not a zero-sum game. One person's gain does not necessarily equal another's loss.

Destructive competition and wars generally stem from fundamentally false beliefs that have been planted deep inside our brains, distancing us from our true nature.

For instance, we often hear the term 'No. 1' bandied about in marketing messages, but in our heart of hearts, if we really listen, we also know that the measure itself is flawed. Reality bears this out time and again.

The best football player may not be the best husband.

The company with the highest revenues may not be the most environmentally conscious.

The singer with the most record sales may have suicidal tendencies.

The country with the highest GDP may have a history of aggression.

The list is endless.

To repeat, the point is not to question the pursuit of excellence and high achievement. It is to question our *motivation* for excellence and high achievement.

Essentially, our yardsticks are faulty and to even begin to understand—much less measure or fight or die for—achievements, we may need to recalibrate the way we look at almost everything.

A good place to begin with is an old concept that is now getting renewed attention: the hierarchy of human needs by Abraham Maslow. It is encapsulated in a pyramid with the lower levels describing basic physiological needs and progressing step-by-step to the ultimate goal of human existence—self actualization.

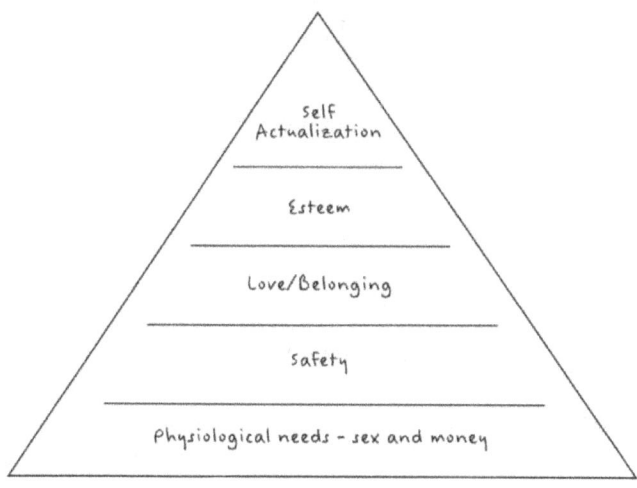

Fig. 1: Maslow's Hierarchy of Needs

In his wonderful book, *Winning the Story Wars* [3] author Jonah Sachs espouses the idea of empowerment marketing. He contends that almost all of the marketing we see today is based on Freudian thought, wildly popularized by his nephew Edward L. Bernays, which is in direct opposition to Maslow's ideas.

While Freud believed that all of humanity spends their entire life in lowest section of the pyramid—dealing with sex and greed—Maslow held out a little more hope for us, believing that we are basically designed for self actualization, the highest section of the pyramid, pursuing wholeness, perfection, justice, richness, simplicity, beauty, truth, uniqueness, and joy.

If all our marketing from the last century or so till today had been based on Maslow's ideas, the world would probably have been a much different—and much better—place than it is today.

Instead, we have walked down the Freudian path, and

almost all of our marketing until recently is based on appeals to the basest of human instincts: greed, sex, money, and power.

Freudian ideas permeated almost every single message ever broadcast over the last century.

How to be more sexy.

How to show off your status.

How to beat your competition.

As a consequence, we as individuals and as a species have fallen far short of the ideal of achievement and human potential that was—and still is—open to us.

Maslow's ideas are creeping into communications today, but Freudian concepts are so deeply ingrained in the marketers' psyches that even when some do take the 'empowerment' route, as many have begun to recently, the noble and inspiring ideas expressed by some of these marketing messages have little real connection with the actual products.

The results are, sadly, shallow at best and deceptive at worst.

To get to where we should have gotten in the first place, we may need to unlearn many of the illusions that have been taught to us, right from the moment we stepped onto this planet.

You probably have experienced this: you hear a tune, and no matter how hard you try to shake it off, you just can't get it out of your head.

Illusions are like that.

And until we snap out of them through deliberate awareness, they continue to silently play in our unconscious, directing our life's path.

To get there, communications in general, and

marketing as a field in particular, really need to be reinvented to accommodate a more holistic view of *why we are here on this planet*. Our existence is much, much more than a series of decisions about what to buy—at least it ought to be.

Life should be guided by the needs of humanity; it is too precious to be molded by the narrow goals of movie makers, advertisers, marketers, social media gurus, and other creators of illusions.

This is not about any ideology. There isn't any '-ism' that can solve the very real problems of the human race. In fact, it is doubtful whether there is any hope for humanity as a collective entity at all.

There is, however, a lot of hope for individuals.

And by a happy coincidence, in today's age of digital communications, for the first time in history, reaching out to seven-odd billion people is actually possible.

5 ILLUSIONS ABOUT ALCOHOL

It was around the year 324 BC in the Persian city of Susa (now Shush in modern Iran). The army of Alexander the Great had just been witness to a bizarre event—an Indian sage, who had accompanied the conqueror on his journey to Persia, had set himself on fire.

The sage was called Kalanos by the Greeks, probably because of his habit of hailing people with the word *kallana*, meaning 'greetings'. Born in Takshashila, home to what is considered to be the world's oldest university, he was 75 years old and terminally ill, and had committed suicide, preferring to immolate himself rather than live life as an invalid.

Much to the surprise of those who watched, not a word of pain or discomfort escaped the sage's lips while he burnt himself. It was this very fearless attitude to life and death, stemming from his deep wisdom, that had attracted Alexander to him and led to his appointment as his spiritual teacher.

It is well known that drinkers are forever on the lookout for an excuse to drink. So, though Kalanos was an ascetic, living on fruits and milk, his funeral was followed by a rather incongruous event—a wine drinking contest amongst Alexander's soldiers.

The winner of the event was a common soldier called Promachus, who consumed thirteen liters of undiluted wine. Three days later, however, he died of alcohol poisoning, along with forty-one other soldiers.

People have been dying of alcohol for a long time. In fact, the first trace of alcohol [4] in human history dates back to around 7000 BC. It was found in Jiahu in North China, made by fermenting grapes, berries, honey, and rice. The word 'alcohol' is derived from the Arabic *al-kohl*—literally meaning 'the eyeliner', due to its original usage in making eyeliners hundreds of years ago.

Today the number of deaths by alcohol poisoning is about one person every twelve seconds—that is roughly the time you took to read the previous paragraph. That currently adds up to about 2.5 million people every year. [5]

It is the highest death toll ever recorded in 35 years. [6]

By the way, this data correlates with the money spent on the advertising of alcohol for approximately the same period, which has also steadily risen, especially through digital communications.

Coincidence?

Not long ago, ads for alcohol would only be found in gentlemen's magazines. Today a teenager is more likely to stumble upon one, browsing the Internet while doing his or her homework.

This is despite the fact the several studies have repeatedly shown that alcohol, along with tobacco, are far more harmful than drugs such as marijuana and LSD. [7] [8]

Public attitudes and government policies towards alcohol and tobacco in most countries are based less on scientific evidence, and more on illusory standards.

SHAKEN, NOT STIRRED

The advertising of alcohol is banned in several countries. Yet one can hardly expect a mere regulation to deter such a smart breed as the marketer.

James Bond has perhaps done more for the sales of the 1969 Bollinger wine and vodka martinis than any advertising campaign ever.

Product placements in movies—which incidentally cost millions of dollars—are the norm today and cut across every product category. Indeed, going by Hollywood fare, one may be led to conclude, for instance, that all laptops are made by Apple, all TVs by Sony, and all successful men drive BMWs.

However, we are not concerned with specific products but rather with the general impact of product placement have on the mind—the world of illusions that forms and crystallizes around them, unconsciously determining the course of our lives.

You probably have seen such scenes scores of times in movies:

The weary hero returns to his room after kicking a gangster's butt or slaying a dragon or whatever.
What is the first thing he does?
Reach for a bottle of Scotch?

The happy heroine enjoys a girls' night out.
They have fun.
What do they do?
Meet at a restaurant?
Sip Margaritas?
Long Island Iced Teas?
Or tequila shots, as a superficial nod to gender equality?

The young boys go out for the first time, part of the ritual transformation of boys to men.

Where do they go for fun?

A pub?

And drink lots of beer?

This insidious marketing of alcohol has been in vogue for decades. Governments too support this, willy-nilly, and you can't blame them because alcohol, along with tobacco, accounts for a sizeable portion of tax revenues—several billion dollars every year.

Not an insignificant amount by any measure.

It may not be conclusive evidence that we have descended from apes but the fact is that we do tend to imitate others a lot, especially our heroes and idols.

Whether we admit it or not is another story altogether, for it flies in the face of our pet illusion that we are self made. So the idea that we are carbon copies is not easy to digest.

Teenagers tend to do this more than the rest of us, perhaps to magically imbibe some of the characteristics or attributes of the hero or heroine, in the youthful hope that some of that stardust rubs off on them. Or perhaps, to expedite the transformation to that exalted state they all aspire to: adulthood.

It's not all James Bond and vodka martinis though.

Many a movie character subtly peddles some form of alcohol.

The regular guy.

The buddy.

The neighbor.

The office colleague.

The boy/girl next door.

So, are they all evil? No.

Is the aura around alcohol an illusion? Absolut-ely.

A famous study [9] by Solomon Asch in 1956 and several subsequent studies conclusively showed that, contrary to our fondly held illusion, human beings are nothing if not imitators.

The test demonstrated that, given a right and wrong option, irrespective of intelligence and education, people will *choose the wrong option* simply because others before them did so—even against their own better judgment and despite having doubts about the choice.

Technically, this extremely strong tendency to conform is called a 'normative influence' in behavioral psychology.

In plainer words, it means we imitate others.

A lot.

It is this normative influence that has given rise to a breed of so-called social drinkers—people who do not consume alcohol when they are alone but 'don't mind' drinking when they have company.

Apart from the movies, the other major contributor to illusions about alcohol is the military.

It is supposedly symbolic of courage, making men out of boys. If you see a hero on screen playing the role of a soldier, you can bet your pension he will have his drinks neat, i.e., without diluting them.

The problem is not that they are all evil folks with a hidden agenda to transform everyone into slobbering alcoholics but that what they sell is an illusion that goes on to color and distort our thinking.

Often they are not just unaware of the illusion but are victims of it—far too many heroes and heroines have succumbed to their addictions themselves.

The concept of Martian thinking [10], referred to by Eric Berne, MD, is the capability to see and hear things without prejudice, in their undistorted form. Martian thinking is to adults what eidetic perception is to children. Alcohol in its many flavors would, in Martian-speak, probably be called rotten vegetable juice. Fine wines and rare whiskies would be extremely rotten juices.

Have you ever wondered why most alcohol brands' logos are extremely ornate and exquisitely designed?

How else could the manufacturers justify some of those outrageous price tags? It's not just the logos—their bottles too are often fine specimens of craftsmanship. The approach seems to be: when you're selling something rotten, you better package it well.

The overwhelming influence of perceived value was shown by a well-known study [11] by Stanford University where participants were given two glasses *of the same wine,* but told that one was cheaper. All of them concluded that the more 'expensive' one tasted better.

In fact, the so-called 'taste' of the more expensive brands of alcohol have more to do with the price tags than any other factor. For a Martian, it is absurd to compare two forms of rotten juices. What do you compare anyway—which one tastes less awful?

But, if it tastes so awful, why do people drink at all? After all, people have been drinking alcohol for a long, long time, and only occasionally for medical reasons.[1]

If drinkers were honest, they would admit that, as the jolly drunkards' saying goes, "Me no drinkee for drinkee, me drinkee for drunkee."

Alcohol has taken root in the minds of many people as the *de facto* norm for social occasions.

Marketers know that people are much more likely to attend a boring event or dinner if cocktails are served. When invitations to such events are printed, they make it a point to ensure that is clearly mentioned on the invitation cards, if not actually highlighted.

If alcohol is *maya*, what is reality?

Social get-togethers of real friends needs no prop from alcohol. We are delighted with each other's company and regaled by tales of achievements and blunders, the natural highs and lows of life.

If alcohol were actually needed to ease the conversation, it probably was not a gathering of real friends to begin with.

From festivals to send-off parties, weekend get-togethers to reunions, no celebration is considered complete without the customary bottle—or crates—of booze.

It is almost like a hefty tax that has to be paid to the alcohol industry for every happy occasion.

Then there is the ice-breaker argument. It is

---

[1] Some forms of medicine do use alcohol, however, its quantity rarely exceeds 1-2 teaspoons at a time. Amusingly, this excuse has been stretched thin by many a tippler who waxes eloquently on the 'medical benefits' of alcohol, usually missing out on the exact recommended dosage, of course.

propounded that in a scenario where groups of people with little in common come together, such as participants at a conference, a few tots go a long way in establishing relationships and smoothening deals.

This works because alcohol shuts down the part of the brain that deals with inhibitions, so we are more likely to talk to people we wouldn't 'naturally' talk to, and say things we wouldn't 'normally' say.

In contrast, take a conference or, more likely, an informal meeting of a bunch of hobbyists or programmers or a group of people following a common passion such as, say, photography.

Photography club members often tend to meet up *before dawn* to catch the best light. Yet nobody complains. (Try holding a pre-dawn business meeting!) On the contrary, everyone at such meets is usually bubbling with enthusiasm about what they do, how they did it, where they went, and so on.

Introductions are made on the fly.

There is a palpable energy in the air.

Connections just happen.

Alcohol is almost never served at such meetings.

What is missing in the first scenario is *passion*.

We do several tasks because we are supposed to, because the job demands it, because the market demands it, or whatever. But because our hearts are never in it, the entire affair at the core is a sham, an illusion.

The solution is not to substitute passion with alcohol, expedient though it may be, but to find that missing passion, and more importantly, figure out why we lost it in the first place.

This is one of the great tragedies of the human condition. The going-through-the-motions to prop up a borrowed notion of success. The human mind and body are capable of much more.

Finally, it is said that people drink to drown their sorrows.

Again, it is the image of the tragic hero or love-struck maiden, whether portrayed through the lens of modern cinema or through tales told by ancient storytellers huddled around log fires, that keeps the illusion alive.

As the saying goes, if your heart is broken, alcohol will heal it in one year. Otherwise it takes 365 days.

The reality is that alcohol does nothing except destroy brain cells, and often makes people say and do things they later regret.

It all has to do with the illusions we have bought into over a lifetime. Very few of us will confess to—or indeed even qualify as—being 'alcoholics' as the term is defined. Most of us, however, will find countless rationalizations against living life without alcohol.

While drinking and its consequences are a matter of personal choice, the Martian approach would be to examine what aspects of our lives are so upsetting, unbearable, or unsatisfactory, that it requires us to go out of our senses to *feel right*.

Overturning a life of illusions, especially those that have been formed over a period of 9000 years, takes courage, clarity, awareness, and time.

REALITY CHECK #3

Here's a seemingly random list of things we encounter in our day-to-day lives. What do these products or technologies have in common?

1. GPS
2. Wristwatches
3. Telegraph
4. Penicillin
5. Radar
6. Microwave ovens
7. Jet airplanes
8. Nylon
9. Canned food
10. SUVs
11. Drones
12. Body imaging
13. Emergency bandages
14. Pen drives
15. Refrigerators
16. Cyber security
17. Digital printing
18. Image stabilization
19. Non-stick coatings
20. The Internet

21. Digital cameras
22. Ambulance services
23. Aviator sunglasses
24. Safety razors
25. Tampons
26. Freeze drying
27. Self-injection syringes
28. Cargo pants
29. Computers
30. Camouflage jackets

All these seemingly random objects and technologies have one rather chilling factor in common: they were all developed so that *we could kill each other more efficiently.* Without exception, each and every one of them was created, advanced, or popularized in the course of military research. In other words, to become better at war.

This list is not exhaustive.

6 ILLUSIONS ABOUT WAR

Thousands of years ago, there was a young prince called Siddhartha Gautama. When he was born, the court astrologer predicted that either he would be a great king or a great monk.

Eager to ensure that he did not renounce the world and his kingdom, his parents, the king and queen, took every care to see that his life was one of joy and beauty. He was never given an occasion to see or hear about anything that may cause sorrow. Till he was a young man, he was kept within the four walls of the palace, surrounded by finest luxuries, wearing the softest silks, eating the choicest food. He did not know about old age or sickness, much less about death.

Yet, though the cage was made of gold, there is nothing even a king can do to shackle human nature.

One night, fed up of being trapped in the palace compound, the prince commanded his charioteer to take him outside the gate.

There for the first time he saw old age.

He saw tears.

He saw death.

It transformed him into who we now know as the Buddha.

That is the impact of the sudden exposure to tragedy on the human psyche.

Contrast that with today's world with its overdose of in-your-face, beyond-your-imagination variety of ultra-violence.

THE (WELL-FED) DOGS OF WAR

Parents, for generations, have screamed themselves hoarse about the ills of the exposure of children to violence in movies and games. There have been shootouts involving teens and pre-teens who went on rampages armed with deadly weapons resulting in senseless deaths. Yet the flood of violent movies and games is growing, not receding. We even have a genre called 'war movies'.

Consider what it has done to our psyche.

Not just the Rambos, their countless sequels, or the World War II 'classics' but going all the way back to over half a century, the novels and comics—the Alistair MacLeans, the Robert Ludlums, and Commando comics. All those stories about the 'heroism' of war. Many of those novels have found renewed life in movies.

This is not to detract in any way from the undeniable courage or unimaginable sacrifices of soldiers on both sides of every battle. If anything, the utter pointlessness of it all only makes it more poignant.

Now try to imagine what it would have been like, how we would have behaved, had we *not been exposed* to our current daily staple diet of shootouts, killings, vile enemies, blood, and gore on movie channels, computer games, and other media.

Is it too far-fetched to assume that, like the Buddha, we too would have been shocked at the very least—if not actually enlightened—by the sight of real war images that were broadcast live, like some macabre entertainment, by some news channels?

Perhaps shocked enough to demand an end to all wars?

We are all potential Buddhas.

What impact would a world full of Buddhas have on governments that thrive on military conquests?

After all, even if we only consider examples from recent history, from the French revolution to the abolition of slavery in the U.S., and all the freedom struggles around the world, one of the latest being the one in Egypt, it is only public opinion that brings real change.

If product placements are the norm for every product imaginable, then is it not possible that even 'war imagery' is just another form of product placement and wars are just the most profitable business of all?

In reality though, all wars are a less-than-zero-sum game, and add up to a loss for humanity, while achieving nothing that cannot be had by peaceful means.

Way back in the 18th century, Samuel Johnson defined patriotism as the last refuge of scoundrels. For centuries, this sentiment has been exploited by rulers and governments to rake up empty nationalistic fervor in their citizens, and then dupe them into meaningless, avoidable—and immensely profitable, for some—wars.

Digital communication has made it a lot easier to misguide millions of people under the illusion of artificial national boundaries, when the reality is that *we are just one people on one planet.*

The effect of the messages sent out by the media is to transform normal, likeable folks into brainwashed, unreasonable bigots. When well-educated people are reduced to baying for blood like savages at the Roman Colosseum, it makes one wonder what education achieves, whether it achieves anything at all.

In *Lord of the Flies* [12], Nobel Prize-winning English author William Golding's gut-wrenching tale about a group of British boys, shipwrecked on an uninhabited island, describes what Carl Gustav Jung in his *The Archetypes and The Collective Unconscious* [13] referred to as the 'veneer of civilization'.

An important component of this veneer is the illusion that somehow war is acceptable.

That it is justified.

That it is for a good cause.

To see the true horror of war, one needs to take off the veil of *maya* that has been constructed around it—the glamour and the glory of battle that are just the stuff of illusion.

During a recent war, at an airport where troops had been mobilized to fly into the combat zone, a connecting flight that was scheduled to take off was running late—a soldier who was supposed to be on board was missing.

Several announcements later, he was found. He had locked himself in one of the washrooms at the airport perhaps for the simple reason that flying into the war zone meant almost certain death.

Numbed by the 'war imagery' fed to us by movies, TV channels, and the media, it is too easy to judge him as a coward.

But perhaps the soldier was a father of a newborn child.

Perhaps he was newly married.

Perhaps he had aged parents to take care of.

Perhaps—there was something about him that only proved he was human.

Some moviemakers tend to take a 'realistic' view, depicting not the 'glory' but rather the horrors of war. Several awards later, however, the movie that results in an end to all wars is yet to be released.

Three centuries before Christ, a king called Ashoka in north India sought to become the supreme emperor of all that he surveyed.

He was stiffly resisted by a feudal lord, Ananta Padmanabha. At the battlefield of Kalinga, their forces clashed and it was a bloodbath. When the victorious Ashoka surveyed the pile of 200,000 corpses, far from elation at his victory, he was filled with remorse.

Not only did he subsequently relinquish all battles, he became a champion for the principles of non-violence espoused by the Buddha.

Getting rid of illusions about war is literally a matter of life and death.

The irony here is that so-called 'action movies' cater to a benign human desire for achievement, excitement, and glory.

Freudians may claim that these movies provide an

outlet for the alleged human lust for blood—the so-called 'instinct of destruction'. Then again, Freud also thought cocaine was good for depression, so it may be advisable to take his readings on human nature with a large pinch of salt.

In fact, most of the advances made in the field of psychoanalysis, which underpins the vast majority of ideas about the human mind—and marketing messages—took place against the backdrop of the World Wars I and II.

Not exactly the most conducive environment if one seeks to study and understand *normal* human nature.

Indeed, it may be argued that formulating theories about the entire human race based on a study of the most neurotic specimens is akin to guessing a person's diet by examining his or her garbage bin.

What human nature really craves is not hatred but love, not blood but adventure, not self-aggrandizement but self-expression. What action movies do is provide vicarious outlets that insidiously *take the place of genuine adventure.*

The common excuse we give ourselves is that our lifestyles do not permit adventurous pursuits often enough, if ever. At best, we opt for adventure holiday packages but mostly, our sedentary lifestyles and jam-packed schedules are directed by our illusions.

What prevents us from living an action-packed life instead?

To live life adventurously is to live the way we lived as children.

To a child, learning to walk is an adventure.

Putting sounds together to form words and stories is an adventure.

Throwing a ball is an adventure.

What prevents us from finding adventure in every moment of every day?

7 ILLUSIONS ABOUT SMOKING

In 1916, in the middle of World War I at Beaumont-Hamel, France, after a bitter exchange of fire, there was a lull in the shooting.

In one of the trenches, a soldier relaxed enough to light up a cigarette. His comrade beside him hissed, "Put that bloody cigarette out!"

The sound of his voice was enough to give away his position. The next moment he was struck down by an enemy bullet.

He was a British soldier, Hector Hugh Munro, better known as an author of dozens of witty and sometimes macabre short stories, written under the *nom de plume*—or pen name—of Saki.

If Saki could, he may well have said of his own death that he was the only man in the world who died because of just one cigarette.

Most smokers die a lot slower and because of a lot many more cigarettes. Tobacco companies, of course, have been even slower still to find any evidence of a correlation between tobacco and death.

WHERE THERE'S SMOKE

The only difference between nicotine and other drugs is that the former is legal. Its advertisement, however, like alcohol, is banned most everywhere.

If you have seen any of the countless heroes and heroines on screen, a cigarette dangling casually from their lips, or chugging away while they work on something terribly important, however, no advertisement is necessary to spell out the message that smoking is cool.

Every single youngster who falls for the nicotine trap has this illusion while they take their first puff of the drug. The fact that nicotine is never overtly termed a drug doesn't make it any less so, it only makes it even more insidious.

Far from eliminating the channels of nicotine distribution, companies are actually multiplying them. So apart from the traditional cigarettes and cigars, we now have nicotine patches, nicotine gum, and electronic cigarettes.

Sure, one of the initial myths is that it is cool. But it is one that every smoker soon grows out of.

Meanwhile, governments walk a tightrope between the staggering profitability of this fatal product and the ever-shriller voices of public opinion.

The statutory warning signs on cigarette packets grow bigger and bigger.

Their messages grow more ominous.

From time to time, advertising agencies release extremely creative advertisements about the perils of smoking.

Many of them go on to win awards.

None of this has any significant impact on sales or profitability of tobacco or nicotine products.

Part of the reason for this is the belief—perhaps deliberate, for it is significant only in the extent that it has been futile—that *providing information* about the harmful effects of smoking is enough to dissuade people from starting or to persuade smokers to quit.

Smokers know every little fact and factoid about smoking—a lot more than any advertising or government agency could ever possibly deign to offer.

It is not due to lack of knowledge that smokers keep puffing.

Just as telling someone several times a day *not* to have a headache is very likely to result in a migraine, telling someone repeatedly not to smoke only *prevents the smoker from forgetting about cigarettes.* It keeps the darn things right at the top of his or her awareness.

Here, we may generously apply Hanlon's Razor, "Never attribute to malice that which is adequately explained by stupidity." So, rather than a malicious corporate conspiracy, maybe the futility of current anti-smoking measures is due to sheer dim-wittedness.

The placement of the messaging is a bit odd though. We see billboards and TV commercials, but rarely a poster at the most critical 'customer touch point' of all—the point of sale, better known to marketers as the POS.

So, the messages seem to appear in media where their effectiveness is minimal or counter-productive: on billboards and TV commercials that merely *remind* smokers about smoking, and on cigarette packs, where it is too late for any kind of messaging anyway.

What's a smoker who just bought a pack expected to do? Read the message and throw it away?

Very unlikely.

So much for the illusion that anti-smoking campaigns do anything. The much bigger—and by far the more dangerous—myth about smoking is that *it is hard to quit*.

In fact, quitting smoking is ridiculously easy.

If stopping smoking is hard, it is only because we view it that way—*because we are led to view it that way*.

The most common illusion among smokers and non-smokers alike is that it takes willpower. In fact quitting needs no willpower at all—it only needs won't power.

A quit-smoking program, also available as a book [14] that has sold more than 20 million copies worldwide and been translated into several languages, Allen Carr's *Easy Way to Stop Smoking* talks about the many myths that keep millions hooked to the nicotine habit. Whether you are a smoker or not, it is worth reading.

8 ILLUSIONS ABOUT RELIGION

Born in 1945 in the village of Satara in India, Narendra Dabholkar was the youngest of ten children of Achyut and Tarabai.

During his growing years he was influenced by modern thought, whilst all around him, the people were steeped in bizarre superstitions and rituals.

He completed his MBBS degree at the Government Medical College and was a medical doctor for over 12 years. The continuing exploitation of the local people by *tantriks*—religious magicians or witch doctors—and self-proclaimed 'godmen' stirred the rationalist in him.

Quitting his practice, he founded an organization for the eradication of superstition and became a vocal champion against irrational practices, directly confronting the so-called holy men, who claimed to perform miracle cures for ailments of a large number of blind followers.

In 2013, he was shot dead.

Four days later, the Indian government passed the Anti-Superstition and Black Magic ordinance.

IN THE NAME OF GOD

Every single religion on earth preaches nothing but love, peace, and the universality of humankind. Yet, throughout history, more people have been killed in the name of God than for any other reason.

Clearly something has been lost in transmission.

If nicotine is a drug that is socially unacceptable then religion is the socially acceptable version. As Karl Marx said, "Religion is the opiate of the masses."

Everyone holds their own personal belief about God.

Some don't believe in the Invisible Man in The Sky but believe in idols.

Some don't believe in idols but believe in a divine presence or pure spirit.

Some don't believe in divinity but believe in cosmic energy instead.

Agnostics believe God is unknown and unknowable.

Even atheists have a belief, which is merely inverted—they believe in the non-existence of God.

All these beliefs are just that—beliefs. And while they all differ, they do have some common threads of *maya* running through them.

It would seem that one of the most widely prevalent illusions is that God can be bribed. This is evident from the fact that several religious institutions rank among the wealthiest organizations on earth with no major source of income other than donations from believers, rich and poor alike.

While it is noble to wish to contribute financially to God's work, all that surplus wealth could perhaps have been put to better use in the service of His or Her children?

Nearly a billion children are going to sleep on an empty stomach, while you are reading this book.

It is unconceivable to think that any divine entity would need a financial contribution from mere mortals. If anything it is a reflection of human fear and greed that presumes that eternal security can perhaps be negotiated for a price.

It's the same Freudian approach to religion that feeds on the lowest segment of Maslow's pyramid, in pretty much the same way as the marketers have done for decades.

Except that with religion, these illusions have been around for millennia. The passage of time has done little to erode these deep-rooted misconceptions that God may be placated by financial considerations to ignore our misdeeds or may give out winning lottery tickets to a chosen few.

It is one thing to build holy places of worship that offer succor but a totally different thing to misuse these places to stockpile enough gold and currency to merit a small army to guard that wealth.

The number of people who subscribe to such illusions is mind-boggling, and many of them are those who can least afford it.

Tragically, this very belief in the Divine is what distances us from the real—for lack of a better word— 'divinity' that exists *within us and all our fellow beings*. Recognizing that well of power would help humanity go much farther than any monetary compensation could. This scarcely understood force is literally the stuff of miracles and fundamentally seems to connect all life on the planet.

In 2015, scientists managed to link 3000 atoms [15], a record number, in a bizarre state called 'quantum entanglement'. Basically these atoms would *stay connected*, even if they were placed at opposite ends of the universe.

The idea had been trashed by Einstein himself as 'spooky action at a distance' which was impossible, but numerous experiments have proved otherwise.

The uncertainty of the position of sub-atomic particles is the foundation of quantum mechanics, on which much of today's technology is based. For instance, the vibration of atoms has been used to develop highly accurate clocks.

What the quantum entanglement experiment proved was that atoms *don't need to be physically connected to have a connection.*

What are human beings, and in fact everything in the universe, if not atoms?

Is it inconceivable that we are all connected on a plane that we simply have not yet discovered?

There is a four-day course conducted by the Isha Foundation at Coimbatore in South India, called the *Bhava Spandana* [16]—literally meaning 'experience the vibration'.

According to a participant, it is possible to actually see one's own physical form as a vibrating mass of energy— outside one's body, within the body of another person.

Sounds really crazy?

Sure, but we cannot be a judge of what we have not experienced. The word *yoga* from Indian spirituality is commonly understood to mean 'union' but perhaps a better translation would be 'empathy'—to be able to feel what others feel.

Maybe, what is really crazy is that, beyond the perceptions of our senses, both modern science and ancient spirituality seem to be heading to a point of convergence, where our beings are in a state of quantum entanglement.

Genetically, humans share about 50% of our DNA with a banana. That means about half of our body has the same stuff that goes into a fruit.

With mice, the similarity is higher—we are about 85% identical to mice genetically, a history going back to a common ancestor 80 million years ago.

We are 90% similar to cats in terms of DNA.

Chimpanzees are 96% identical to us.

And when it comes to humans, all of us are 99.9% identical to each other.

The so-called differences between humans—race, color, and what not—account for just 0.1% of our DNA.

Is 0.1% worth fighting and killing for?

Awareness of our commonalities is several millennia old—a Sanskrit phrase, found in ancient Hindu texts such as the *Maha Upanishad*, refers to humanity as *Vasudhaiva Kutumbakam*, which means 'the world is one family'.

Against this backdrop of fundamental interconnectedness, the very concept of competition for survival or achievement between human beings is ridiculous. When we compete against each other, it is the right hand wrestling with the left.

In the context of religion, this means that the very notion of 'different' Gods needs to be relooked at.

PROFITING FROM DIVISIVENESS

Consider the three major religions of the world: Christianity with 2.2 billion followers, Islam with 1.6 billion, and Hinduism with 1.1 billion.

All over the world, you will find vested interests that focus on the differences between these religions, to the extent that for centuries, blind followers of each religion have been led to zealously wage wars on each other. Few, if any, studies, are conducted or popularized that focus on finding common ground among them, though one has to merely scratch the surface to find similarities.

For starters, the names of the very fathers of these religions, Abraham, Ibrahim, and Brahma are too similar to be a coincidence.

The fact is that there are narrow interests in keeping humanity divided in the name of religion—and nationality, and gender, and politics, and race, and sexual orientation, and income levels, and a whole bunch of stuff that can fill another book.

Once upon a time, two cats chanced upon an *appam*—a sweet delicacy made in South India. You only have to taste one to understand why the cats were so excited.

Now those two cats believed in sharing, and so decided to divide the *appam* into two equal halves. They proceeded to tear it into two pieces, but as luck would have it, the two pieces were not equal.

They had a long argument, with neither willing to concede, so they finally took the two unequal pieces to a wise monkey.

The monkey took one look at the pieces, and came up with an instant solution. With the consent of the cats, he took one bite of the larger piece so as to make them both equal.

As it turned out, the monkey took too large a bite, and now the pieces were still unequal, and the cats were still unhappy.

The monkey happily obliged, and took another bite from the bigger piece, which again resulted in two unequal pieces.

And so it went, till the cats were left with nothing, and the monkey had swallowed up the entire *appam*, burping contentedly.

While this seems too childish a tale, it is this very

principle that enabled the erstwhile British empire—the so-called *raj*—to hold sway over much of today's 'developing' world for centuries.

When two people fight, it's a third party that profits. The idea of the 'separateness' of our identities, especially our religions, is one of the biggest illusions we need to overcome to make the world a truly better place.

9 ILLUSIONS ABOUT PROFITS

Thousands of years ago, four young Brahmin lads from a village in India decided that they'd had enough of the rural life. They wanted to see the wide world, find adventure and riches.

Setting out on their journey, they traveled far and wide, only to discover that wealth only came through effort.

Tired and weary, having found neither wealth nor adventure, they finally came upon an old man, meditating under a tree. With kindness in his eyes, he asked the four friends what brought them into the wilderness.

Upon hearing their story, a smile crossed his face, and he spoke, "You're in luck, lads." Reaching into a small package beside him, he pulled out four cotton wicks and, handing one to each of them, continued, "Follow your heart with this wick in your hand. Where the wick falls, you will find the treasure you seek."

Thrilled to bits, the lads, with new found energy, continued their quest. Soon enough, the first lad accidentally dropped his wick. Furiously the four began to dig with whatever rocks and sticks they could find. In minutes they struck a rich vein of copper ore. Bundling up as much as he could carry, the one who dropped the wick said, "There's enough money to be made from selling this. Let's go back home."

The rest had other plans. "What is copper worth? Nothing! Let's head further," they choroused. But the first was content with what he found, and went back home.

Some way ahead, the second wick fell. This time they hit a cache of silver. Again, the second took what he could carry, and headed back, while the remaining two trudged on.

After a while, the third wick fell and this time they hit pure gold. Taking all he could carry, the third decided to head back, and did his best to convince the fourth, "Look, this gold is more than enough for both of us for generations to come. Let's not get too greedy."

His friend would not budge, "The next wick is bound to fetch us diamonds. What's gold compared to diamonds? I'm going on, with or without you."

On he went, and some way ahead, came across a strange and horrifying sight—a man standing, covered in blood, with a wheel whirring on his head, while he struggled in vain to stop it with his hands.

The fourth lad went closer and blurted, "What the heck happened to you?"

The moment he spoke, the wheel flew from the victim's head, and landed on his own. He shrieked in agony, "Get this off me!"

The victim, now a free man, told him, "I can't. Like you, I too came this far because I wasn't happy with copper, and silver, and gold. When the next greedy man comes along, you will be free. Goodbye!"

"Wait, how long will it take?" asked the fourth guy.

"I don't know. Time stops when you're suffering. All I remember is that when I got here, the Buddha was alive."

This ancient tale is relevant in today's world of stock busts and financial institutions that are deemed 'too big to fail'.

THE BIGGER THE BETTER

Most of us automatically subscribe to the illusion that companies need to grow. More and more and more. After all, how else will the poor things survive, right?

Not quite.

To survive and even thrive, the only thing a company needs is to make profits. So why do companies that *already are profitable* need to grow at all?

As a company's growth is defined by the amount of market capitalization—the total value of its shares—when a company grows, its share prices go up. So the major reason for growth is not a real demand for more products by *customers* but an insatiable demand for higher stock prices by *investors*.

Most investors try to 'get in' at the early stages of a company's formation, when there is a lot of potential for natural, organic growth or even explosive, exponential growth.

Once its natural growth tapers off, however, there is not much more money to be made and that's when the tail starts wagging the dog. Investors then need to *manufacture growth* to squeeze every drop of profit out of the company.

Even marketing guru Jack Trout, in his incisive bestseller, *In Search of the Obvious: The Antidote for Today's Marketing Mess*, [17] plainly states that growth simply isn't a goal worth pursuing.

The desire for *artificial growth* is at the heart of much of the marketing illusions being created today. And they thrive on the ignorance of most people about the jargon that is casually thrown about.

For instance, an analogy to the 'credit default swaps' that caused the financial bust of 2008, would be a car salesman telling a customer, "Hey look, here are some cars that are quite likely to crash on a highway with you inside. How many of them would you like to buy?"

The response to the bust, euphemistically termed 'quantitative easing', printing trillions of dollars for the institutions *that caused it*, is as insane as awarding the Nobel Peace Prize to Hitler.

In the online space, it gets even wackier.

Several billion-dollar valuations of well-known (obviously!) companies are based on parameters that can be termed shaky at best—the estimated lifetime value of potential future buyers, for instance. Marketers will be quick to further obfuscate such terms with jargon such as ELVs and PFBs, giving scornful looks at anyone who confesses ignorance about them during presentations.

Translated into Martian, the ELV of PFBs means that the company's value (the price at which it is bought and sold) is decided based on sales *it has not yet made* to customers *it does not yet have*.

Wow!

Since the whole scenario is illusory, what is the poor marketer to do? Get everyone, or at least as many people as possible, on board to buy into the illusion.

This distorts the natural supply-demand curve and it is no longer a free market but a *forced market* situation. In a world suffocating from junk, surely the very last thing that is needed is a concerted effort to create more of it.

Great companies will grow *because* they are great companies.

One of the biggest illusions is that all companies need to grow. They don't.

They only need to be profitable.

Anything beyond natural growth, through business excellence and great products or exemplary service, is just greed. And as Mohandas Karamchand, better known as *Mahatma*—meaning a great soul— Gandhi said a long time ago, there is enough for human need, but simply not enough for human greed.

10 ILLUSIONS ABOUT TIME

It was late in the morning. The man, a leader of his people, was heading to his office. He had been suffering from dizzy spells but was hardly one to let such a trifle stop him from conducting his affairs.

A bigger worry was the dream—or nightmare—that his wife had been having of late. In her visions, she saw his life in great danger.

That morning, she pleaded with him to stay at home. His best friend and ally, who was at his side, put his hand on his shoulder and asked him whether he was the kind of man who would pay so much attention to a woman's dreams.

That subtle prod at his 'manliness' was enough. He made up his mind and went along with his friend, ignoring the pleas of his wife.

Minutes later, the same friend and ally, stabbed him in what became infamous—after western history's first recorded post mortem, incidentally—as 'the unkindest cut of all'.

The year was 44 BC. The man was Gaius Julius Caesar.

Several centuries later, another leader of his men, had a

premonition about his own death. He shrugged off his dream though it irritated him.

Before retiring for the day, he wished his bodyguard, a certain William H. Crook, with the words, "Goodbye, Crook."

According to the bodyguard, this was the first time he used the word 'goodbye'. His customary greeting was, "Goodnight, Crook."

Later that night he was shot.

The leader in question was Abraham Lincoln—incidentally shot to death by a person who he admired.

The common question in both these tragic stories is this: how did they know in advance about the assassinations?

RUNNING OUT OF TIME

In Lewis Carroll's timeless *Alice In Wonderland*, the wild White Rabbit says, "The hurrier I go, the behinder I get," but today, time-saving devices seem to make a lot of sense.

Do they really?

Suppose we're walking on the road, and pass by a group of about 20–30 people. A bus arrives and all of them get on board. Would we follow them because, surely, taking a bus is faster than walking?

One would hope not.

After all, we have our own destination, our own purpose, and wouldn't get on a bus simply because it is faster or because other people are doing it.

That would be stupid. Right?

But take a look at a very short, random list of time-saving devices and tools we all use:

Baby food
Ready-to-eat meals
Microwave ovens
Email
Mobile phones
Instant tea/coffee
Shorthand

It would seem that shortly after we are born, we get on a whole bunch of bus rides, without any more compelling reason other than that they are faster, and everyone else is doing it—and are not in a position to get off.

It's even been nicely packaged for us in the phrase, 'the need for speed'.

We are led to believe that 'the pace of life has changed', that we live 'in the fast lane', that 'you need to move fast', that 'nice guys finish last', and so on and so forth.

Who coins these catchphrases and introduces them into our lexicon? And what purpose do they serve?

About the only thing they have achieved is to create a plethora of need-for-speed-related diseases, all of which come with a hefty hospitalization bill: heart disease, asthma, obesity, depression and anxiety, gastrointestinal problems, and Alzheimer's, to name a few.

If we really look at those random time-saving inventions, we will find little to enrich our lives, and perhaps a lot of reasons to minimize their use, if not to avoid them altogether.

Baby food—whatever it was that babies ate before

baby foods were developed, it seemed to have worked quite well for thousands of years, without any need for this particular product category.

Ready-to-eat meals—the nutritional value of packaged food, with or without preservatives, is questionable and it just may be better to skip a meal than eat out of one of these packets.

Microwave ovens—the jury is allegedly out on the effects of radiation on food, but don't expect to hear from microwave oven manufacturers any time soon.

Email—most people's days begin with a pile of unread emails. Time saver? Really?

Mobile phones—these were invented for battlefields. Is that how 'normal' life is supposed to be?

Instant tea/coffee—if one has ever tasted one of these vile concoctions, nothing more needs be said.

Shorthand (now defunct)—this was a squiggly language used before speech-to-text and doesn't exist anymore. Thank heavens for that, but we all have our own forms of shorthand for taking down notes in a 'time crunch'.

Our general approach to time is quite similar to dogs barking up the wrong-est of trees. What's really behind most, if not all, time-savers is a faulty mindset born out of *maya*. Perhaps it is not time that needs to be saved, but our lives, because of the way we live.

Whether we are individuals, businesses, or countries— if we want to get anywhere, what is more important than the need for speed is the need for a *destination*, a purpose that is worth our limited time and our precious life.

And just as nine gynecologists cannot help a pregnant woman deliver a baby in one month, when we're creating something worthwhile, we need to wrap our brains around the fact that it may take some time.

Research into why the *Ashoka* Pillar, an iron structure at the Buddhist site of Sarnath in North India that was built more than 2250 years ago, has not shown any signs of rusting revealed that its construction was an extremely time-consuming process. Not 'commercially viable' today.

There seems to be a direct correlation between the quality of a product or skill and the time poured into its creation, which is *intuitively evident to the human mind.*

Beyond this illusion of saving time, however, is the grander—perhaps the grandest—illusion of time itself.

For starters, does time actually exist?

Is there any such reality as a present, past, and future? Just because we wear watches, does it bring some entity called time into existence?

What we call time is the directionality of physical, chemical, and biological processes—while modern thought believes time to move constantly forward, many ancient cultures tended to believe in a circular notion of time. Irrespective of what we believe, time is just that—a belief.

People grow old.

Things wear out.

We perform different actions when the sun, moon, and stars are at different positions.

None of these events really proves that time exists. Perhaps the root of this illusion is that time is equated with other concepts in physics such as gravity.

Gravity *causes* us to fall down to the ground.

Time, on the other hand, *does not cause* us to grow old.

To try to define time it is like a trying to lift ourselves by pulling on our feet with our own hands. Physicists have been at it for ages, and recently, an elite gathering of scientists [18] debated for four days and couldn't really come to any consensus on the physics of time.

The lack of a proper understanding of time hasn't stopped us from going even further—many people have debated on whether time travel is possible.

'Time machines' have been part of immensely popular works of science fiction, from H.G. Wells' *The Time Machine* and Isaac Asimov's *The Second Foundation* to Douglas Adams' *The Hitchhikers Guide to the Galaxy* and the Hollywood flick, *Back to the Future*.

One of the stumbling blocks against time travel has been that, according to Einstein's famous equation, $E=mc^2$, or energy equals mass times the square of the speed of light.

In plain words, this means that time travel would require an object to move faster than light, which would result in its mass shooting up to infinity—in other words, beyond a certain speed, the object would explode.

But this Hollywood-ian line of thinking presupposes that we need a person or an object, *having mass*, to travel. So the real question is—what does time travel actually mean?

If it is merely a question of 'perceiving' the future or the past, then all that time travel requires is a 'perceiver'.

This inextricable link with the perceiver is a conundrum of modern science, while ancient mysticism faces no such issue.

It all began when Newton came up with his laws, which

worked fine when dealing with falling apples and large objects, such as planets and cats—the macroscopic world of 'classical physics'. Problems started to show up when sub-atomic particles—the microscopic world—were discovered.

To explain the behavior of these particles like electrons and photons, physicists came up with 'quantum physics'. The problem was that classical physics couldn't co-exist with quantum physics. When one worked, the other had to go out the window.

The absurdity of trying to combine the two types of physics was demonstrated by a famous thought experiment, Schrödinger's cat.

According to quantum physics, sub-atomic particles can potentially have different states at the same time—called a superposition. So for instance, light particles can be waves or particles, depending on how you look at them.

Schrödinger hypothesized that if we put a cat in a box with a vial of poison gas that either gets released or not, depending on a quantum particle, it means that the cat is also in a state of superposition. In other words, until we open the box, the cat is *both dead and alive.*

Such paradoxes probably arise because modern science approaches the truth from the outside-in whereas spirituality works from the inside-out.

In science, the observer and the observed are always two separate entities—there is the scientist and there is her lab. When a scientist observes the universe, however, such separation is meaningless, because *the scientist is part of the universe.*

As mystics put it, "Who will know the know-er?"

To get back to our 'perceiver' of time: our senses of perception are what define our reality. We define reality according to how our brain interprets what we see, hear, smell, taste, and touch.

This 'perceiver' is unencumbered by mass and gravity, so it can theoretically travel faster than light without worrying about its mass shooting up to infinity and exploding—because it has no mass to begin with.

Now consider the phenomenon of *clairvoyance*, where people see flashes of the future, such as Calpurnia, Caesar's wife and Abraham Lincoln.

If the entire universe is just a vibration, as proposed not just by ancient mystical thought but by modern string theory of quantum gravity, what we perceive as reality—that is, the present moment—is basically an intersection of the present vibrational state with our perceptual lens.

Maybe, traveling back and forth in time is a question of a 'perceiver' intersecting with different vibrational states, from the 'past' and 'future', in much the same way mobile phones pick up frequencies?

Maybe, as Magnon, the Emperor of the Galaxy, told Mandrake the Magician, the fastest thing in the world is not light, it is thought.

Whether all this is possible or not, what seems certain is that 'defining time' and 'traveling in time' are impossible when our minds are obsessed with 'saving time'.

Paradoxically, to move faster than light, we may first have to learn to slow down. It is one thing to be punctual, and quite another to let our lives be dictated by clocks.

11 ILLUSIONS ABOUT FOOD

Mothers are the embodiment of caring—generally speaking. With Little Tyke it was the opposite.

Little Tyke's mother was filled with rage at her newborn.

Why wouldn't she be?

In seven years, her modesty had been outraged over and over again with surgical precision. Each time she became pregnant and delivered, she was filled with loathing for her babies. She felt what any mother may feel at that unwanted piece of life.

Utter revulsion.

Raging, uncontrollable fury.

But she did what mothers don't usually do. She grabbed her babies by the neck, crushing them, and flung them to their death.

She did this with every single one of her babies. Little Tyke would have met the same fate, had it not been for the fortuitous presence of Georges and Margaret Westbeau at the zoo that moment.

The mother, a glorious African lioness, had flung Little Tyke, its newborn cub to the other end of her cage.

Reaching through the steel bars, Georges and Margaret

quickly rescued the injured cub from certain death.

Slowly they nurtured the tiny beast at their farm, the Hidden Valley Ranch near Seattle, U.S., till it was in perfect health. Whether it was the violence of its birth or the company of the other farm animals—horses, cattle, peacocks, cats, and dogs—is not known but Little Tyke developed a peculiarity unheard of among lions.

The lioness was a *vegetarian.* [19]

No amount of coaxing and cajoling could make the animal consume a piece of flesh or a drop of blood.

If a full-grown, 10-foot-long, 350-pound lioness, classified as an 'obligate carnivore'—a creature that cannot survive without meat—can turn into a complete vegetarian, then surely it is a lot easier to influence the diet of human beings.

What influences our diets?

Many would say that it is our location, and what food our parents cooked, and what their parents cooked before them. Indeed, recipes are often passed on from generation to generation, as part of—sometimes closely guarded—family traditions.

But that just kicks the can further down the road. It doesn't answer the question: why do we eat what we eat?

WHAT'S ON YOUR PLATE?

Food is one of the big obsessions of today. If a lot of the messaging we are flooded with today is related to food, it should be no surprise, because food businesses are one of the most profitable—to those running them, of course.

Nature in its infinite wisdom provides for all living creatures, exactly according to their environments.

So camels have humps.

Giraffes have long necks.

Why should humans be different?

Our bodies are best suited for food grown in our climates and environments, what is available in our localities.

Even the seasons dictate what crops and fruits grow, and eating healthy to a large extent is as simple as just staying in harmony with nature's rhythm.

Yet, one characteristic of our eating habits today is that much of our food comes to us from far and wide. It is fashionable to try out exotic dishes, vegetables, and fruits, sometimes flown to our table across continents.

It would be interesting to ask how much of this taste is related to the food itself, and how much is due to the illusions created by *food-related messaging*. The biggest example of this is champagne and caviar—that epitome of fine dining.

Just as our body tells us when we are thirsty, it also tells us what kind of food to eat. It does require a certain level of sensitivity and awareness, however, to distinguish what is a genuine demand from our biological system, and what is an illusory mental craving created by marketing messages.

If much of what passes off as food today is probably far from nourishing, it could be because another characteristic of our food is that, quite often, it is cooked by perfect strangers.

Any great chef will tell you that *love and caring* are perhaps the most important ingredients of any recipe—we are all familiar with 'grandma's apple pie' and 'the way my mother cooks'.

On the other hand, most restaurants today are mass-producers of a commodity that is passed off as food with the primary aim of making a quick buck. It is not fast food but fast money—most restaurants operate at a minimum of 300–400% profit margins.

Love and caring rarely, if ever, come into the picture—never mind what the corporate slogans say.

The third monster in the kitchen is GMO—genetically modified organisms.

Nicknamed 'Frankenfoods', these fruits and vegetables have found their way into the daily diet of people globally—and, in the absence of GMO labeling—without their knowledge. [21] [22]

Labeling—or the lack of it—is only one of the issues with GMO.

Creating GM seeds, for instance, interferes with the natural process of pollination, leaving farmers worldwide at the mercy of a few multinationals. [23]

Pesticide resistance induces farmers to use even more pesticides on crops.

The most misleading of all the marketing messages around GMO is the philanthropic spin doctoring that it will help in solving the world's hunger problem.

The reality is that there is *no shortage of food*—the problem lies in the cost of *distribution* of the food that *already exists*.

If all the food in the world were to be evenly distributed, every single person of the over seven billion on the planet would have more than enough calories everyday for proper health and nutrition.

One-third of the food produced today is simply wasted—thrown away or left to rot.

Do we need to *increase* food production at all in the first place, let alone through GMO?

The fourth food-related issue is that soon, ironically, approximately two out of ten people in the world will be obese, while another two out of ten will be starving.

In other words, 20% of the people who need food are starving not because there is no food in the world, but because they don't receive the food that is already produced. At the same time, 20% of the people who do receive food will fall ill *because* of the food they get.

There is something in the way we treat nature's bountiful blessings that is making us seriously ill. It is common knowledge that fruits are great for health: "An apple a day…" You rarely hear of someone who ended up with an illness caused by eating fruits. Yet the sugar extracted from the same fruits and plants has created one of the biggest killer diseases of today, diabetes.

It is—or should be—generally accepted that the farther removed a food item is from its natural form, the less beneficial it will be and yet we are consistently fed—no pun intended—illusions like the one about sliced bread being the greatest invention of mankind.

Some of the sugar-free options being sold in some parts of the world today to diabetics can cause illnesses that are even worse than diabetes itself.

It is more than the mere lack of nourishment in the food we eat. If 20% of the population is going to be obese, not only are they eating the wrong food, they are eating a whole lot of it.

One of the possible reasons for this is that the human

brain confuses boredom with hunger. What do we tend to do if we have nothing else to do—at least the more fortunate among us? Watch TV—and munch on something?

What is it that makes life so boring in the first place that we need to *eat our way* out of boredom, to find some excitement and fulfillment.

Can it be that the flood of marketing messages has created such a distance between us and reality to the extent that we are no longer aware of how we feel, what we eat, or what it really does to us?

We are the same smart people who wouldn't get on a bus just because others were doing it. Yet we get taken for many rides every day.

The fifth aspect of our feeding habits today is the concept of cooking and re-heating food using microwave ovens. While there are some Swiss, German, and Russian studies on its hazards [20], one may find little other conclusive research to prove the detrimental effects of microwaves on the molecular structure of food—a process rather appropriately called 'nuking'.

You can conduct a small experiment of your own and decide for yourself.

REALITY CHECK #4

Make a simple dish in a microwave, and then make the same dish in the 'traditional' way.

So, if you eat eggs, try making two omelets, one in a microwave and the other in a frying pan. (Vegans can try eggless puddings.)

Heating by microwaves involves violently vibrating every food particle at a molecular level till its temperature goes up. Do we need a scientific study to guess that maybe, just maybe, this might distort the molecular structure of the food, and possibly affect its nutritive value?

Just compare the taste of the two omelets, or puddings, and decide for yourself whether any further scientific research is needed at all.

12 ILLUSIONS ABOUT WATER

In a sleepy village on the outskirts of Mumbai city in India, near a church built by the Portuguese in 1840 is a government-aided convent, St. John the Evangelist High School. Till the late 1980s, the kids returning home from school would get a quick, free-of-cost refill of their empty water-bottles at a little shack that passed off as a restaurant.

In the 1990s all that changed with the invasion by bottled water and cola companies, and with it the phobia—another marketing *maya*—that not only was bottled water safe and absolutely necessary, it was fashionable.

Semi-naked models quenched their thirst on the front pages of mainstream newspapers.

The villagers wondered how they survived without it and very soon, everybody and their aunts were drinking only out of plastic bottles, instead of the ubiquitous steel glasses they were used to. Concerned mothers advised their kids to buy bottled water, the very next day after they had—safely enough—drank 'regular' water from the little shack.

Not only did bottled water and sodas wipe out the livelihoods of the local lemonade and ice candy stalls, they transformed the naturally generous restaurateurs—whose doors were always open to quench the thirst of the school kids and passersby, free of cost—into evil little monsters who now sought to make a buck out of thirsty people.

Meanwhile, several tons of fresh plastic waste pile up in the oceans [24] and in developing countries every day. [25]

The body adapts to consume food and water from its locality. That's why tourists tend to fall sick after drinking the water while local residents never do.

If anything, what was needed was to improve the local standards of hygiene and quality of water being served.

A BILLION LITERS OF WATER

One famous bottled water manufacturer proudly claims that, through rain water harvesting, they put back as much water as they consumed.

How nice of them!

The depletion of groundwater levels and subsequent droughts, however, seems to suggest that such claims are dubious at best. Besides, was consuming *billions of liters* of water necessary to begin with?

Of course, the same manufacturer is mum about the unaccounted-for, billion-odd tons of plastic waste it generates.

Or about all the fuel it burns to transport water around the world? [26]

Wouldn't it have been better for the people and the planet they purportedly care about to just implement rainwater harvesting? By actually contributing to society, they could have added some substance to their multi-billion dollar 'social' media campaigns.

Water—in its unpolluted form—has enough minerals to meet human needs, especially the humans in the locality.

The simple alternative to the illusion of 'mineral water' is a process invented thousands of years ago, which incredibly, still works—boiling! Boiling kills all germs that could possibly be detrimental to health, and it preserves all the natural minerals and nutrients that we need, which incidentally bottled water does not, not to mention the side-effects of the, well, 'minerals'.

Stand-up comedian, George Carlin, once said that we concern ourselves too much with plastic waste. The earth would simply shake off human life like a dog shakes off fleas. Indeed, an increase of a few degrees in global temperature is all it would take to put a conclusive stop to all grandiose human endeavors.

Looking at the tragic spate of tsunamis, cyclones, and floods around the world, it would seem that nature has begun the process.

Incidentally, these are not the rants and ravings of 'green terrorists', but findings by the Earth Science Communications Team at NASA's Jet Propulsion Laboratory in the California Institute of Technology.

To put things in perspective, during the Ice Age, when the northeast United States was covered by more than 3,000 feet of ice, average temperatures were only 5–9°F lower than today. [27]

The effects of global warming, degree-by degree, are ironically rather chilling.

An increase of about 2°F is enough to make life hell and 5–6°F higher temperatures would end life altogether—that's basically our grand children we are talking about. [28]

Do we *really* need billions of plastic water bottles so badly?

The obvious, in-your-face solution is to prevent water pollution in the first place. What companies around the world need to do, to genuinely 'win the hearts and mind of people'—the holy grail of marketing—is to invest in providing and ensuring clean drinking water, on tap, for the local populations.

The social media campaigns will then take care of themselves.

No clever slogans required.

13 ILLUSIONS ABOUT POLLUTION

In 1858, a Bavarian couple, Elise and Theodor gave birth to a boy they named Rudolf, the second of three children. By the age of 14, Rudolf had decided that he wanted to be an engineer. Armed with a scholarship from the Royal Bavarian Polytechnic of Munich, he studied at the Industrial School of Augsburg.

After an experiment with steam engines using ammonia almost killed him, he turned his attention to other forms of engines. Due to his knowledge of thermodynamics, he knew that high pressure could be used to attain very high temperatures—high enough to ignite fuel. (It is the converse of this principle that causes temperature in empty space to fall as low as -455 °F.)

Not only was Rudolf successful in developing an engine based on high compression, he was a bit too successful.

His engine was based on peanut oil and was much more efficient than any other engine at the time. He acquired patents to manufacture them in Germany and the U.S. and hoped to replace steam and combustion engines with his design, which ran on the same principle as the much-touted bio-fuels of today, except that he was more than a century ahead of his time.

He dreamed of a world where peanut farmers would co-exist with engine manufacturers and more importantly, his fuels were environmentally safe and produced zero pollution. In 1913, he boarded a steamer, the Dresden, to attend a meeting in London.

He never reached there.

Days later his body was found floating in the North Sea in Norway. The engineer's name was Rudolf Christian Karl Diesel and his invention is well known as the diesel engine of today.

What was a dream of having an environmentally safe product—peanut oil—was rudely cut short, leaving humanity stuck instead with a nightmare called gasoline or petrol.

To add insult to fatal injury, instead of using peanut oil, the diesel engine was then made to run on a by-product of gasoline that was highly toxic, and generally hated by everyone. As a final nail in his coffin, this filthy product was christened 'diesel'.

For a very long time, the very word diesel was looked down upon, another sad illusion created by marketing.

The rest as they say is—a very tragic—history.

SOLVING THE WRONG PROBLEM

In 1997, the Kyoto accord got 192 countries to agree to reduce carbon emissions with a view to containing climate change. Today, we all love our cars and as conscientious folks do the best we can to keep our emissions under permissible limits.

Except that the real problem with cars is not the pollution caused by *driving* them, it's the pollution caused by *manufacturing* them in the first place.

Depending on the model of the car, manufacturing one vehicle releases between 6–35 tons of carbon dioxide [29]. And that's a conservative estimate because it's too complicated to account for the carbon footprint of every single part that goes into a car—tires, paint, electronics, plastic, nuts, bolts, iron ore, and so on, besides the fuel for shipping parts across the globe.

That's *before* it hits the road.

The local drunk once lost his car keys in a pub. Some hours later his wife, concerned that he hadn't returned home, set out in search of him, and found him standing under a street light, desperately scanning the pavement.

When she asked him what he was doing, he explained that he had lost his keys. Further investigation revealed that they had fallen from his pocket, when he took a tumble, some distance away in a dark alley.

Throwing her hands in the air she asked him why on earth he was looking for them on the pavement if he dropped them in an alley.

He replied, "Because this is where the lights are."

Idiotic as it may seem, this strongly resembles our approach to vehicular pollution.

THE ROAD AHEAD

The biggest challenge is that we have fallen too deeply in love with our cars. If you've seen the 1968 Walt Disney movie, *The Love Bug* or the more recent 2006 movie, *Cars*, who can be blamed for falling in love? It's an affair that begins from the time we are children.

Yet, the belief that we are doing our bit by reducing exhaust gases is an illusion. For instance, in the U.S., the greenhouse gases produced by an average family of four by eating meat is more than that produced by driving two cars. [30]

The concept of collective ownership, leasing and renting vehicles may go some way in reducing the glut of vehicles on the market. What we really need to do is stop manufacturing and buying up more cars—or at least stop kidding ourselves.

14 ILLUSIONS ABOUT PRODUCT INNOVATION

Born in Afghanistan to a Turkish warlord and his aristocratic Persian wife, Mahmud of Ghazni was one of the most prominent rulers of the Ghaznavid empire. In thirty odd years, he had conquered most of what is modern Iran, Pakistan, Afghanistan.

Amazed by the gold and precious jewels he saw in northwestern India, he vowed to raid and loot the wealthy region every year. True to his word, he invaded it as many as seventeen times, each time pillaging it for its riches.

His richest hauls were from the fabulously rich Somnath temple in the Indian state of Gujarat. He only plundered the temples, making no attempt to annex them, probably to prevent the source of his riches from drying up.

All his wealth, of course, did not make him less mortal, and he died in 1030 AD.

It is said that his dying wish was for all his wealth to be displayed before him, and with tears in his eyes, he asked for his most precious treasures to be buried with him.

Long before him, another conqueror, Alexander of Greece, had a similar wish—he wanted the path to his grave to be strewn with all his gold, silver, and precious stones.

We may not possess the wealth of Mahmud and Alexander, but when it comes to amassing stuff, we are on the same ride.

THE PROBLEM WITH MOORE'S LAW

Whether one has heard of Moore's Law or not, all of us have certainly experienced it—it states that computing power of electronic devices doubles every 18 months. This translates into a new model of mobile phone, laptop, or such gadget popping up in the market even before we pay off the monthly installments on the previous model.

To anyone marketing such devices, this is a whopper of an opportunity.

To the buyers of such devices, and the planet in general, this is a whopper of a problem.

Do we have any idea what happened to our very first mobile phone or computer?

Or the second?

Or the third?

They are all still around, and will be around long after us, like ghosts created by a species obsessed with technology.

Some of them lie in little-known garbage dumps—euphemistically called 'landfills'—dotting the planet, some will be exported to developing countries, and the rest will end up along with the millions of tons of garbage floating in the oceans, that we never get to see, leeching chemicals that will find their way into groundwater, and eventually poisoning ourselves. [25]

Sure, it is nice to have a device that works faster, but the ridiculous irony of Moore's Law is that, most of the time, to most of the people, most of the computing power that these devices provide is useless.

Most of us simply do not need machines that are so powerful.

This has given rise to an entire industry of 'thin client solutions', which are based on sharing the excess computing power of devices among multiple users.

If we are not one of those who wait for days and nights in serpentine queues, waiting for the first day of a new, over-hyped product release, chances are our devices will be obsolete soon after we buy them.

This is another one of the buses we get onto, because we feel that we cannot afford *not to*, because everyone else is on the same ride.

Through media and social messaging, we are made to feel ashamed if our laptops are 10 mm 'thick', when the newest model is only 5 mm 'thin' or some such nonsense.

We are made to feel somehow inadequate if our TV screen is not flat, or curved, or does not support 3D, or HD, or super HD, or ultra HD, or whatever.

We are made to feel pre-historic if the ringtones on our phones aren't polyphonic and sound like, well, a phone ringing.

It's all about the way we are made to feel.

And our kids are born into this world of technology, plugged into headphones before they can even learn to speak.

Mobile phone radiation has been known, though it is not publicized enough for obvious reasons, to cause insomnia, confusion, and headaches.

Dr. Devra Davis, an epidemiologist from Johns Hopkins university and internationally recognized expert on electromagnetic radiation from mobile phones and other wireless transmitting devices, has conducted various studies that demonstrate a correlation between wireless radiation and testicular dysfunction, breast cancer, childhood brain damage, and dementia. [31]

In the hurry to 'go-to-market', most technology and software companies opt for phased releases—in other words, launching a half-baked product that isn't quite perfect. Some of the wrinkles get ironed out in the next 'version'. And the next, and so on. So instead of just one great product, the market is flooded with never-ending versions of products, each one supposedly better than the previous.

Saying that the new version is better is just another way of saying the previous version sucked, but that isn't the issue. It's the line of thinking—why sell just one product when you can milk the people by selling multiple versions to the same buyers?

Over and above this, products are ill-designed to last very long anyway, which makes it easier for people to 'upgrade' to the next version. There are a lot of adjectives to describe owning these devices, but 'smart' isn't one of them.

In *The Story of Stuff*, Annie Leonard, one of the prominent voices against mindless overconsumption, opines that we need to stop thinking of ourselves primarily as consumers and start thinking and acting like citizens. [32]

In fact, we need to go a step further, and think not as citizens of artificially created borders but as citizens of the planet, as co-creators in a fundamentally interconnected universe.

Arthur William Radford's words on art are even truer of technology: "Half of art is knowing when to stop."

To know when to stop, we need to first think about people as human beings rather than 'consumers'. The effect of this utterly disempowering term is to conjure an image of human beings as some sort of voracious, insatiable, 'productivores', instead of sensible, intelligent beings with infinite potential.

It is well-known that Einstein came up the theory of relativity, but what is less known that he was awarded the Nobel Prize *not for his theory* but for something relatively mundane: discovering the photo-electric effect—a *commercial* application, not a 'mere theory'.

This summarizes the banal approach towards products that is so common. It is not about the magnificence of the creation, but what price it will fetch on the market.

15 ILLUSIONS ABOUT CAREER

If you've ever played a game of cards, you owe a hat tip to the grandfather of all card games, an English gentleman by the name of Edmond Hoyle.

Born in 1672, Hoyle's rules of card games made him a legend in his time and for centuries afterwards. His first publication on the rules of whist in 1742, *A Short Treatise on the Game of Whist*, was so successful that it went on to become one of the earliest books to be pirated.

He went on to write numerous other best-sellers, on the rules of chess, probability theory, and backgammon, among others.

Sure, they became authoritative references but one may ask, what's so noteworthy about a bunch of books about cards and board games?

Not much.

What is noteworthy, if you noted the year of his birth and the publication of his first works, is that when he wrote his first best-seller, *he was seventy years old*.

That's when most everybody gets firmly settled into retirement.

So, what did Edmond Hoyle do before he became the guru of games?

Nobody knows.

And *that* is the difference between following a career and following one's calling.

If many more of us did what we really loved, or liked, or were *really* good at, the global job market would be quite different from what it is. We need much fewer bankers, businessmen, engineers, and marketers, and many more poets, painters, musicians, sculptors, and sportspersons— and card players.

THANK GOD IT'S FRIDAY

If we were to ask any employee of any company how happy they were with their careers, it's likely that most would reply with some degree of positivity.

But rephrase the question, and ask them if they prefer every working day of their life to be like Monday morning or Friday night, and it's almost certain that every single one would choose the latter.

What's going on?

It would seem that behind the more-or-less happy faces of their careers lurks a deep longing to be—somewhere else.

That's the reason folks such as the intrepid blogger, Steve Pavlina [33] who created *Personality Development for Smart People*, and Robert Kiyosaki, [34] best-selling author of *Rich Dad, Poor Dad*, are staunch believers in never ever taking up a job.

The illusion behind the quest for 'secure' jobs is our insecurity. We feel that we don't have a choice. What fuels this myth is the most primal—and crippling—human emotion of fear.

The truth is that if we are capable enough to be employed, we are capable enough *not* to need a job—if only we could shed our fear.

Yet, the world over, countless people spend long hours, weeks, months, even years away from their families and friends—people whom they love the most—for their work, and in perhaps the greatest irony of all, they do it *because* they love them the most.

One of the factors behind this voluntary, schizoid behavior is the skewed model of development that is followed globally, where the focus is on mega-businesses, mega-cities, and mega-nations. The reason for this model is purely economic, but the human cost is too much to bear. Happiness is not measured in spreadsheets and presentations—it is in spreading love and being present.

In this digital age, localized, decentralized, globally distributed development is easy to achieve. What is only needed is for ever greater numbers of people to shed their illusory fears.

As a result of this fear, people, especially the youth, tend to sacrifice their passions at the altar of success. The price they pay in the pursuit of an illusory standard of a 'worthy' goal is the time they spend, which can never be retrieved.

Every day youngsters choose finance over fine arts.

MBAs over music.

Sales over songs.

CHASING FOOL'S GOLD

There's a guy, let's call him Jack, who graduated in chemical engineering, got a doctorate designing reactors, and finally worked for a software start-up, in the retail sector, developing websites.

What was his passion?

Playing the drums.

Jack is not the exception but the rule. The quest for illusory success makes people do crazy things—*which are all considered normal.*

Mark Zuckerberg, the co-founder of Facebook is considered one of the most successful young entrepreneurs of our age. Books have been written and movies have been made about his strategies and life, how he got there, what it takes to succeed, and what lessons may be learned from his story.

The real reason for his success is actually quite simple. Clues can be found in the results of a study that began a long time ago—the Harvard Study of Adult Development [35], which began in 1938, and was one of the most comprehensive longitudinal studies in history.

As part of the study, which lasted 75 years, psychologists measured the 'happiness level' of 268 undergraduates from across all strata of society. They concluded that there are only two factors that ultimately count: having someone who will be there for us no matter what happens, and having healthy social relationships.

In other words, connecting with loved ones and having social relationships are the lifetime goals *of all humanity*—and that is what Facebook taps into, simply and elegantly.

Is it any wonder then that social networks have been such runaway successes?

Incidentally, the principles that made Facebook and many other social networks successful *do not apply* when using social networks for business.

As many social media 'experts' are finding out, despite pouring billions of dollars into social media campaigns, they fail to plug into a corresponding strong and relevant human need. In other words, people use social networks for, well, social networking, not doing business.

At the end of the day, if we have someone who loves us, and a bunch of jolly good friends, our life is successful. And that is all there is to it.

Unless driven by the need for self actualization, everything else we 'achieve' is a complete illusion, which will provide little fulfillment beyond placating our often fragile egos, and is a complete waste of our limited time and precious lives.

16 ILLUSIONS ABOUT EDUCATION

Cricket and baseball have much in common. A bowler or pitcher throw a ball. The batsman/batswoman/batter hit it and run to score. Beyond these obvious similarities is the role of mathematics behind the bowling/pitching.

Differential equations are one of the more dreaded topics in mathematics. They are used to describe curves such as semi-circles, squiggly lines, the orbits of planets, the trajectory of space rockets—and the path of a moving ball.

The ball always follows a curved path in three-dimensional space, and so, requires a three-dimensional mathematical equation to describe its journey from the hand of the bowler to the bat.

Moreover, since the ball takes a few milliseconds to make this journey, time is also a factor in the equation.

Therefore, describing the movement of the ball will require three variables—x, y, and z—to denote its position in three-dimensional space and another variable—t, for time—for the exact time at all points on the path.

If that wasn't complex enough, weather conditions, wind speed, the condition of the ball, and—in the case of cricket—the dampness of the ground further complicate the path the ball ultimately traverses.

When the batter strikes the ball, what he or she does—in mathematical terms—is to solve a complex equation to find the value of four variables—x, y, z, and t—*and* make some engineering calculations to account for wind and weather, to figure out where to position the bat at what exact instant, so as to actually connect the bat and the ball.

In an interview, one of the greatest batsmen of all time was asked if, sitting at the top of his career, he had any regrets. He replied that he did have a major one. As a child he was very poor in studies, which was a big disappointment to his father, a teacher. He regretted it deeply. His worst subject was mathematics.

Poor at mathematics?

Here was a guy who had mastered every stroke in the game and scored more runs than anyone in history. In mathematical terms, he could solve third-order differential equations more accurately, elegantly, and *faster than anyone else in the world.* And yet he felt he was poor at math.

When we don't know *what* we know, it is a pretty sad state of affairs.

WHEN KNOWLEDGE ADVANCES—BUT WISDOM LINGERS

Ask someone if, given a pen and paper, they can solve differential equations, they will in all probability say, "No!" Unless they are teachers or students of mathematics.

Ask them if they can catch a ball thrown in the air and, in all probability, they will say, "Yes!"

But, if you know to catch a ball thrown at you, not only

are you solving a complex differential equation but you're doing it mentally and in real time.

The truth is, *even dogs know* how to solve differential equations.

Over a century ago, Bernard Shaw quipped that what we want is to see the child in pursuit of knowledge, not knowledge in pursuit of the child. Going by the state of schools and colleges in the world, we still haven't learned the lesson.

And the reason why the current educational system, almost everywhere in the world, fails to bring out the best in students is that *it never has been the goal.*

Education today aims at ensuring uniformity, not developing individuality. How can we put a bunch of children—potential musicians, painters, engineers, mathematicians, surgeons, poets, and scientists—in the same room, and *grade them all on the same test?* Yet that is precisely what education does. Standardized testing is the holy grail of the educational system. There are a few exceptions such as the Montessori and Waldorf schools but they are just that—the exceptions.

The illusion here is that education prepares the young for life. In reality, the majority of schools and colleges merely prepare youthful minds—like lambs to the slaughter—for the cross that most will bear throughout their lives: their jobs or in more dignified terms, their careers.

The objective of education is to help unwitting youngsters to qualify to wear that badge or name tag. Most youth simply do it because adults tell them to and adults know better.

Do they really?

Most adults are as clueless about the purpose of their lives as youngsters. At least youngsters have the confidence of youth. From working fixed hours and wearing uniforms to following rules and doing mindless tasks, the similarities between school life and typical employee life are too many to be coincidental.

The idea here is not to create rebels but to celebrate individuality.

It is not to condone indiscipline but to foster inventiveness.

It is not about creating conformity but encouraging the questioning of everything—a natural tendency of uncorrupted human minds.

The fact is such development of individuality and questioning of authority may be essential for individual growth—but they are certainly not profitable for businesses and wars. And that is what fundamentally defines the educational systems today, and is responsible for the utter stupidity of most curricula at all levels of education everywhere in the world.

To revisit the story of Jack, the guy who studied how to design reactors but actually loved to play the drums, he once spoke up to his boss about changing certain business processes in his organization to improve efficiency.

His boss' immediate reaction was to fire him.

So much for independent thinking in the corporate world. This isn't the norm, thankfully, and most organizations would have given Jack a raise or promotion or both.

By and large, however, schools *are* designed to produce an unquestioning and compliant bunch of conformists.

Kids have a habit of asking questions to the point of irritation. Yet it is that very questioning that defines our humanity. The image of an exasperated parent or teacher, nagged by a child's incessant questioning, telling them to shut up, is almost a cliché.

What happens is that eventually, the children *do* shut up.

They shut their mouths as well as their minds, and end up being almost sub-human for that.

It calls for an almost superhuman level of patience in the teachers, and a supportive educational system, to keep that curiosity alive in all children, for it is their very birthright.

When our schools produce compliant children, they grow up into unquestioning adults. This lack of questioning is responsible for many of the things that are wrong in the world today.

What keeps conformity alive is simply this—it is profitable.

To repeat, the idea is not to create a horde of rebels, or incite non-conformism for its own sake. Rather it is to encourage what may be termed a scientific temper or an attitude of curiosity—a natural state for human beings, until they get educated.

In fact, even the act of rebellion has been hijacked by the primary creators of modern *maya*, the marketers. When you think of rebels, what are the images that come to mind?

Youngsters with bad haircuts?

Garish tattoos?

Body piercings?

Harley Davidsons?

In fact, what is considered rebellion is merely an inversion of conformity—it is basically *conforming to an illusory image of rebellion.*

True rebellion is a Copernicus daring to say that it is the Sun, not the Earth, at the center of the universe. It is a Galileo saying that Copernicus was correct—though he was later intimidated into retracting his statements.

How many Copernicuses and Galileos have been stifled by the moronic educational systems around the world? And to what end, except that it is more profitable.

In an absorbing speech at a Technology, Entertainment, Design conference—better known as TED talks—an English teacher, Sir Ken Robinson, asks whether schools actually *kill* creativity [36]. For anyone even remotely connected with education, and that should include everyone, it is worth watching.

While no one—not even an engineer—is likely to remember the generalized solution of differential equations, anyone who has learned cycling will never forget it, though it is a more complex activity, requiring not just cerebral activity and muscular coordination but courage and tenacity as well.

If differential equations were taught on the cricket, baseball, or soccer fields, it is unlikely that anyone would ever forget how to solve them. Nor that any math class would ever be cut.

And if bicycling was taught the way we teach differential equations today, it is equally unlikely that anyone in the world would ever learn to ride a cycle in their entire life.

17 ILLUSIONS ABOUT GENDER EQUALITY

A 26-year-old villager in north India had little luck in romance. He wasn't all that well-to-do but did his best to make himself attractive to women. He wore the most fashionable clothes he could afford. He tried to speak and appear knowledgeable and intelligent.

None of his efforts brought much success.

In 2002, he came across an advertisement for a deodorant on TV. The saucy commercial led him to believe that merely spraying the perfume on his person would result in pretty females flocking to him, much like bees to flowers with honey.

Seven years and several hundreds of cans later, he was still without a single date.

Finally it dawned on him that he had been had, and in 2009, he took the company to court, demanding £26,000 from the manufacturer for the 'depression and psychological damage' caused by the product.

Luckily for him, the court ordered him to be recompensed for all the money he spent.

While that villager may have been deluded to an extreme degree, so is everyone of us, to varying extents.

The famous Dove commercials did take a step forward by exposing the deception behind those impossibly good looks of fashion models, and encouraging women to be themselves. It will take more than just one company, however, to overthrow many centuries of being objectified.

KEEPING UP WITH THE TIMES

The progression of fashion trends over the last half a century in say, trousers or jeans has roughly been as follows:

1960s—narrow bottoms
1970s—bell bottoms
1980s—tight fits
1990s—baggies
2000s—comfort fits

Curiously, one never could take an item after it went out of style, and alter it to match the next trend. In other words, the only choices we had were to:

(a) Dump all our old stuff and buy new clothes.
(b) Look hopelessly outdated.

Try walking around in public wearing baggy jeans today and a few snickers are practically guaranteed.

Is it surprising then that fashion is a multi-billion dollar industry?

First of all, where are the rules of fashion written except in what *everyone else* is wearing?

Secondly, does it make sense that people of vastly

divergent body shapes and structures could ever fit into a similar type of clothing? Yet all over the world, every year people religiously try to fit into a new set of clothes that most of their bodies were ill-designed for. Often, this is at the expense of more traditional clothes that offer the flexibility to adjust the fit, in perhaps another example of illusions promoting conformity over individuality.

Fools and their money are soon parted—and probably there's no fool like a fashion-conscious one. In fact, fashion-*consciousness* is actually a form of unconsciousness, and a very profitable one for the seller.

For the buyer, mostly, the craving to be fashionable is symptomatic of a deeper—and natural—longing to be accepted, to be recognized, to be adored.

Unfortunately, contrary to the myth, fashion is a very poor, shallow, and unfulfilling substitute for genuine recognition. Even Gianni Versace advised fashionistas not to be into trends.

Yet it is very much to the benefit of fashion labels to keep the customer feeling unhappy and unfulfilled with themselves, in a perpetual state of tension and nervousness about their appearance.

Unhappy customers try—are *led* to try—to find happiness by buying things. In advertising circles, this is cloaked in yet another fancy label, 'aspirational messaging'.

Many people are surprised to learn that even the most gorgeous movie stars, without hours of make-up, look like—surprise, surprise—normal human beings.

The saddest part of these illusory good looks is that many women buy into them too.

By accepting that women are objects, they *participate* in the sordid drama that has kept them at the receiving end of gender inequalities for way too long.

India is a country that produces many curiosities—one of them is a kind of music called *bhangra* rap. It consists of pulsating, and loud, drum beats typically played by Punjabi farmers in North India, coupled with a *masala* version of African American rap music. Some people find it irresistible, while others equate it with a form of torture.

Decades ago, when the music video of one of the most popular songs of this genre was being created, it was the among the first animated ones in India, a fact that was completely lost on the singer, whose only query was, "Where are the girls?"

Semi-naked, of course.

Ironically, in North India, if one had suggested using his mother or sisters as models, one could have got killed.

Men do women the greatest disservice of all by promoting their objectification.

In the days before politically correct terms such as 'chairperson' were coined, there was a knock on one of the hostel room doors in an engineering college campus.

The inmate, bugged at being woken up from his siesta, asked gruffly, "Who is it?"

In reply came a soft, female voice, saying, "Post*man*."

His ear for incongruity perked him up, and now wide awake, he asked again, "*Who* is it?"

Again came the reply, "Post*man*", in a voice as feminine as could be.

Flinging the door wide open, he saw it was indeed a woman, come to deliver the mail. When he asked her how she could call herself a post*man*, she had no reply, except a mumble to the effect she was just doing her job.

The point is though we are careful to avoid gender biases, with terms such as 'chairpersons', and 'spokespersons', referring to 'actresses' as 'actors', with probably 'person-made disasters' next in line, it all amounts to little more than paying lip service to women.

For all the political talk and global wars about American 'freedoms', it should boggle the mind that not a single woman has ever been at the top leadership position in the U.S.

In modern history, the countries that have or had female heads of state include Argentina, Austria, Bolivia, Burundi, East Germany, Ecuador, Finland, Georgia, Guyana, Haiti, Iceland, Indonesia, Ireland, Latvia, Liberia, Malta, Mongolia, Nicaragua, Panama, Philippines, Sri Lanka, and Switzerland. Even such obscure nations such as Tannu Tuva, Guinea-Bissau, and San Marino, and China, much maligned for its lack of freedom, have had women leading them.

The countries that have or had female heads of government are Australia, Bahamas, Bangladesh, Bulgaria, Burundi, Canada, Central African Republic, Ceylon (now Sri Lanka), Croatia, Denmark, Dominica, Finland, France, Germany, Greece, Guinea-Bissau, Guyana, Haiti, Iceland, India, Jamaica, Latvia, Lithuania, Lithuania, Macedonia, Madagascar, Mali, Moldova, Mongolia, Mozambique, Myanmar, Namibia, New Zealand, Northern Cyprus, Norway, Pakistan, Peru, Poland, Portugal, Romania, Rwanda, São Tomé and Príncipe, Senegal, Slovakia, Slovenia, South Korea, Thailand, Transnistria, Trinidad and Tobago, Turkey, Ukraine, United Kingdom, and Yugoslavia.

Some of these are countries that most people did not even know *existed* yet they are advanced enough to vote women into power. So there is certainly no lack of precedent for women at the helm of state affairs, if at all one was needed for a self-proclaimed champion of 'freedoms'.

Genuine consideration for the equality of women would begin not with hypocritical labeling but with equal pay and equal rights, and most of all, doing away with the objectification of women.

For instance, the mere existence of that so-called epitome of fashion, the Miss Universe and Miss World contests, nullifies any illusory gains created by coining gender-neutral job titles.

In the 1980s, their marketing arms attempted to pre-empt feminist objections to such pageants by doing what they do best—coining an empty slogan: 'beauty with a purpose'. To date, what the exact 'purpose' of parading women on stage in their underwear is supposed to be remains unclear.

Decreasing popular support has led the organizers of such demeaning contests to take their wares, along with the manufacturers of equally obnoxious concepts such as cheerleaders, to gullible—or indeed, pliant—developing countries.

From their very childhood, girls are subconsciously encouraged to participate in the illusion that females are objects, by participating in unspoken 'competitions' of beauty at schools and colleges and in communities, and trying to live up to illusory ideals such as the one that the Dove commercials tried to bust.

The sooner such illusory ideals are dismantled and put away, the better the chance to bring about real equality between the genders and provide women a fair opportunity to express their very real talents.

18 ILLUSIONS ABOUT HEALTH

The 200,000-line *Mahabharata*—meaning the epic tale of the *Bharata* dynasty—is the longest poem ever written. Set around 2500–3000 BC, it is an account of the 18-day war between two families, and has come to epitomize the struggle between good and evil.

While pre-natal or in-utero learning—the knowledge imparted to a child while still in the womb—is still a topic of debate today, the *Mahabharata* describes perhaps the earliest recorded case of this kind. [37]

According to the story, while Abhimanyu, the son of Arjuna, one of the main characters, was still in his mother's womb, he heard his father talking about *vyuhas*, or military formations. Specifically, he 'learnt' about how to penetrate a *chakra vyuha*—a circular, maze-like formation designed to trap any particularly bothersome enemy soldier.

It is a labyrinth made up of seven concentric circles of soldiers in a pattern that is not visible from the ground, making the formation impossible to detect until is complete, and too late for the target.

When Abhimanyu was sixteen, he came face to face with this formation in the battle of Kurukshetra (near modern New Delhi in India), and rushed headlong into it, secure in his capability of breaking through it.

However, in the womb, he had only heard his father talk about how to get in, and not how to get out.

So when his fellow soldiers were prevented from rescuing him, he was completely trapped inside, and soon met an untimely end.

What was true thousands of years ago is still true— incomplete knowledge can be fatal.

THE BUSINESS OF HEALTH

Fitness has become the rage everywhere. One can't walk a hundred meters without some sort of fitness-related messaging slamming us in the gut.

People are getting extremely serious about fitness and announcing it too. We can wear our fitness on our wrists. We can even share—or show off, if possible—our 'fitness scores' on social media.

For a bunch of people who are so obsessed with fitness, however, we are more unfit than ever before, if the hundreds of billions of dollars that countries spent on health care last year is any indication.

How come?

There was a time, not so long ago, when the mere word 'nursing' would immediately conjure an image of Florence Nightingale, the persona of *The Lady with the Lamp* making her rounds, attending to wounded soldiers at night.

Somewhere down the line, however, health care stopped being a profession and became an business.

The conversion of health care into a source of profit makes you wonder: whatever happened to the one of the world's noblest professions? Of course, this is not to say that there are no selfless individuals anymore—countless medical researchers, doctors, and nurses the world over who continue to dedicate themselves to the service of the ill and the injured are testimony to that.

Apart from the sheer obnoxiousness of seeking to gain from a fellow being's misery, one of the main issues with the business of manufacturing and selling pharmaceutical products is that what was considered a wonder drug today may quite easily be banned tomorrow.

In contrast, ancient systems of health such as *yoga* and *Ayurvedic* medicine have remained unchanged for thousands of years.

Doesn't that make one wonder?

To begin with, most of the illnesses that require a 'fitness intervention' are caused by defective lifestyles and diets.

Those advertising agencies that market health care one moment will, in the next, market products that promote the very lifestyles and diets that cause those very health problems in the first place.

Secondly, it is a common misconception that fitness is a purely physical phenomenon.

In reality the physical body is, metaphorically, blanketed by layers of thoughts, emotions, and pure energy, all of which equally need to be 'fit' for the term fitness to have any meaning.

If our thoughts are disorganized, fitness is a joke.

If our emotions are not in our control, fitness has no meaning.

If our biological energies are not in harmony with the nature that created us, fitness is impossible.

The reason the 'physical fitness' illusion can be

perpetrated is a deep ignorance of how life works.

Most fitness goals today focus on achieving a certain number: body mass, fat percentage, weight we can lift, miles we can run, mountains we can climb, height we can jump, or some such *quantity*. This is just looking at the tip of a rather large iceberg. It is not possible to reduce human health to a single, or even a set of numbers.

One day, returning from math class, a student complained to his parents that it was impossible to learn the subject because the teacher kept changing her mind.

Further investigation revealed that the teacher had once declared that x+1=4 and hence x=3. The next day she said x+2=3 and therefore x=1.

What was the poor kid to believe?

Just like that student who couldn't pin down the real value of 'x', how can anyone strive to achieve fitness when there are as many fitness 'systems' as there are days in a year?

Consider for instance the proliferation of diets and exercise routines that keep changing every other day.

Pilates or HIIT?

Atkins or South Beach diet?

What system do you follow?

Even a rather simple system such as yoga has been mutilated beyond recognition with the active marketing of terms such as Hot Yoga, Power Yoga, Yin Yoga, and heaven-knows-what-next.

To perform yoga to the accompaniment of loud music and thumping beats, or indeed any music at all, is an aberration beyond words, a grotesque personification of ignorance, and takes the essence of yoga way out of its original context.

You may use a violin to hammer nails into a board, and it may even work, but that doesn't mean that is what violins are supposed to do. Yet that is exactly what most of today's 'yoga systems' are about.

All these systems focus only on the physical aspects of fitness, whereas a holistic system considers stability and harmony as the central themes of genuine fitness.

The 'original' yoga—which literally means 'to unite' the body with the energy of the universe—is a holistic view of the human system, and has little to do with body contortions.

It is unknown exactly when the yogic system was created. What is known is that it was compiled by an Indian sage called Patanjali, around 400 BC.

His eight-fold path comprised about 196 *sutras*—or principles—encompassing the physical, mental, emotional, and biological energy aspects of life and provided a path to transformation, a roadmap to fulfilling one's life purpose.

A brief look at the eight steps should provide some insight into the expansive scope of a truly holistic approach to health, fitness, and beyond. All steps need to be approached with an attitude of love and reverence, an inner seeking, and not with a sense of hurry to 'achieve a goal'. Without love there is no yoga.

The eight steps are:

1. **Ethics** *(Yamas)*—The foundation of health is ethics, honesty, non-violence, moderation of sexual desires, and avoidance of possessiveness. This has little to do with morality. Purity is our nature and external concepts of morality only serve to contaminate our essence and confuse our minds.

2. **Discipline** *(Niyamas)*—The second component of health in the yogic system is discipline and contentment, and contemplation of one's thoughts. Here, discipline is not something to be enforced externally, but rather by getting in tune with our natural rhythms.

3. **Posture** *(Asanas)*—The third aspect of health is the ability to *comfortably* hold different body postures, with much attention paid to the spinal posture that is fundamental to a healthy body. Many of today's 'yoga courses' focus only on this aspect, but it forms only a small part of a much bigger whole. The aim of *asanas* is to rectify the specific postural defects of an individual, usually caused by years of imbalanced sitting, standing, walking, or sleeping. It is a kind of medicine. The *asana* that is prescribed for you may not be the right one for me. Teaching a similar set of exercises to everyone is just another example of mindless conformity. Incidentally, comfortably holding a single pose is enough. It really isn't necessary to learn a whole bunch of them.

4. **Breathing** *(Pranayama)*—The fourth part of health in yoga is the regulation of the breath. The breath is the barometer of emotions, and while our emotions are reflected in the way we breathe, the converse is also true. Thus breathing provides a thread to gain control of our emotions, and by regulating the breath, one can regulate one's emotions too, which is one of the foundations of modern spiritual programs such as the *Sudarshan Kriya* [38] and Inner Engineering Programs. [39]

5. **Awareness** *(Pratyahara)*—This is the beginning of one's inner journey, going beyond physical health

to the cultivation of awareness, and the detachment of the mind's attention from illusory distractions.

6. **Focus** *(Dharana)*—This is the amplification of one's mental faculties to develop a laser beam-like focus through concentration and introspection. It enables one to unravel a lifetime of thoughts, like picking out individual strands of spaghetti that have formed and solidified over the years. Through this unraveling, our thoughts stop of their own accord, *without any effort*, and we are free of illusions and ready to experience reality.

7. **Meditation** *(Dhyana)*—This is a deeper level of single-pointed contemplation on any idea or object, it doesn't matter what. When the thoughts drop away, the canvas is empty, the gates of consciousness open, and the majesty of reality hits us in all its beauty and splendor. We empathize with all that exists, and feel at one with the universe.

8. **Salvation** *(Samadhi)*—This is the ultimate level, the purpose of life according to yoga. Having experienced all there is to experience, a person decides to 'leave her or his physical body' at will.

So there is a lot to be addressed for any system to be *complete* and fulfill the purpose it sets out to achieve—'total health' or 'complete fitness' or whatever term the marketers come up with next.

This is a far cry from what is actively marketed—and sold at exorbitant prices—as yoga, in the name of fitness and health.

Most modern 'yoga systems' focus purely on the performance of *asanas*—body postures—and purport to magically deliver health and fitness.

To believe that one can be healthy merely by wringing the body through complicated contortions, however well-intentioned, is an illusion beyond words.

The approach to health today—especially adopted by those in the business of selling health insurance—seeks to convince us that our body is a delicate and fragile mechanism that needs to be continuously monitored and regularly checked up to ensure that it isn't falling apart. These messages use the factor of fear to sell a whole bunch of unnecessary products. "Over 40? Time for a complete checkup," they proclaim. Yet even those over 80 can do just fine if we live right, and there lies the proverbial rub. Most of us are confused as to what 'living right' even means.

In reality, the human body is a powerful and resilient machine, with incredibly sophisticated senses.

For instance, our sense of touch has a sensitivity of 13 nanometers—that is 0.000000013 meters [40]. For perspective, a hair is about 0.0001 meters thick, and a red blood cell about 0.000008 meters.

Our eyes have the ability to distinguish 10 million colors [41].

Our noses can distinguish 50,000 different scents. [42]

Our bones are stronger than concrete and steel. [43]

One look at the years of systematic abuse that many of us put our bodies through, in the way we work, eat, drink, smoke, and live, and it is evident that it is nothing short of a miracle that our bodies continue to function at all.

Given the right environment—mental, physical, emotional, and spiritual—our systems are designed to deliver perfect health for a very long time.

Can we imagine ourselves being fit enough to climb a mountain when we are 80 years old?

Probably not.

Yet that is very easy to achieve when our *approach* to

health is complete.

Much of our health—and illness—begins with our thoughts, our food, and our lifestyles. The illusory, *manufactured tendency* to focus too much on diseases and ailments only serves to bring them into existence. There is no magic system or diet or workout—and certainly no magic pill—that can ensure perfect health, other than to consider life as a whole.

19 ILLUSIONS ABOUT APPEARANCES

In the late 19th century, a British army major stationed in India, who was very fond of dogs, was transferred to a different part of the country.

He telegraphed the stationmaster of the newly formed Indian Railways to ensure that his beloved Labradors were safely transported to his new destination.

As chance would have it, the lock to the cages in which the dogs were kept was rusty, and the Labradors, five in all, escaped *en route*.

When the train arrived with the empty cages, the stationmaster realized that his career was on the line. Quick-witted chap that he was, he quickly rounded up five stray dogs from around the locality and put them in the cages, and delivered them to the major.

When the major, not unexpectedly, raised hell, the stationmaster, pulling out his booking register, flipped it open and, taking a deep breath, explained with a straight face, "Sir, see here, five dogs booked."

He then pointed at the cage and continued, "And see here, five dogs delivered."

While it remains unknown whether the stationmaster got away with it, many product marketers today routinely get away with such sleight of hand.

WHAT YOU SEE ISN'T WHAT YOU GET

How many times have products failed to meet the expectations created by their packaging?

The most disappointing examples of this kind of letdown—nothing short of deception—are encountered with confectionery and chocolates. The packages and the advertising conjure images of mouth-watering treats that the contents seldom match.

Such misleading examples are not restricted to food alone by any means:

Cosmetics.
Automobiles.
Electronics.
Financial products.

You name it. They all have their share of misleading information and/or imagery.

You can recognize them if you look carefully, for even marketers are not above the law, and need to confess to their deceptions, which is done via carefully worded phrases, almost always in fine print in some obscure corner of the message.

"Creative visualization."

"Under controlled test conditions."

"Results may vary."

"Subject to this-and-that."

Government bodies most everywhere come up well-meaning regulations on paper to plug every loophole, and marketers most everywhere simply find more devious ways to circumvent them. The approach of the creators of such less-than-subtle sleight of hand seems to be to treat people with disdain, secure that they will still continue to consume their products. This security has a short shelf life, and all it takes is *one competitor* who delivers what is promised on the carton to put them out of business.

It is this factor alone that has been behind Dove's meteoric rise to global leadership. In the age of digital communications, marketers who ignore it do so at their own peril.

Albert Einstein was a person who paid scant attention to the quality of his clothes. When his wife pointed out that his clothes were too shabby for one of his standing, he reportedly replied, "What a tragedy if a package of meat was worth more than the meat itself."

How many times have *we* purchased something based on an alluring image?

That's the power of *maya*.

In her own way, Einstein's wife was correct. Even a man of his caliber could be judged negatively because of his appearance. We place too much importance on appearances, far beyond the dictates of hygiene and good grooming.

On the other hand, in some areas of our life, many of us do expect—in fact, demand—complete compliance between what is promised and what is delivered. One such area is our relationships. There would be hell to pay if one of the partners discovered some 'fine print' about the other, that was not divulged in advance.

Why don't we hold our relationships with product manufacturers to the same standards? After all, as advertising legend, David Ogilvy said, "The customer is your wife."

Even from a financial point of view, we spend as much, if not more, on products in our lifetimes than we do on our spouses.

The reason we have such different standards is something we have looked at before—we imitate others. So, we don't complain because *nobody else does*.

Of course, it's not that we don't complain at all. We do, when the products we paid for are defective or don't fit or don't work the way we expected. Rarely, if ever, do we complain about products that don't match their illusory advertising claims. In nearly three decades, for instance, I'm yet to hear about a single complaint that the amount of filling in cream biscuits is nowhere near what is brazenly depicted, right on the package itself.

We seem to have fallen into an unconscious state of quiet despair, and simply have got into the inertia of settling for less. Ultimately, whether it's products or spouses, the quality we get depends on the standards we set for ourselves.

20 ILLUSIONS ABOUT ATTENTION SPANS

In the 19th century Wild West, there lived an old chief of the peace-loving Hopi tribe, who was legendary for his capability to remember and keep track of the minutest details.

His fame reached the ears of an American cowboy, who then decided to put the chief's talent to a test. He made the journey to the chief's *tipi*—or tent—and informed him of his intention.

The chief graciously agreed.

The cowboy rattled question after question, about names, dates, facts and figures, and the chief answered them with amazing accuracy. Finally, the cowboy asked, "What did you have for breakfast twenty years ago?"

"Eggs," came the reply.

Convinced about the chief's prowess, the cowboy left.

After wandering around the land for twenty years, chance brought him back to the same area once again.

Wondering how the chief was doing, he decided to pay him a visit. When he reached there, he saw the chief sitting in practically the same position he had left him in, all those years ago.

He greeted the chief in the traditional way, "How!"

Without batting an eyelid, the chief replied, "Fried."

WE'RE LESS ATTENTIVE THAN GOLDFISH

In recent years, marketers would have us believe that most everyone has been afflicted by a mysterious disease called 'diminishing attention spans'.

How did this happen, we wonder.

And we are told that it is all the rapid bombardment of information that we go through, that our poor brains' attention spans crumble and fall below that of goldfish, and soon perhaps, butterflies.

In reality, it takes one of today's largest supercomputers *forty minutes* to accurately simulate just *one second* of human brain activity. [44]

Maybe, we only pay a few seconds' attention to marketing messages because *that is all they are worth*.

The problem, then, is not in any dramatic fall in the users' intellectual capacity but in the quality of messages they are forced to put up with.

The next time someone tells us that the attention span of human beings has dropped to eight seconds or less, we need to politely inform them that the sale of books by *just one* online bookseller in the past year was over $5 billion. Presuming that the books were bought to be read, the buyers' attention spans would need to extend considerably longer than eight seconds.

Far more likely, nothing is wrong with our attention

spans.

It's not just hapless marketers who contribute to the deluge of dubious content. The digital era offers everyone including pre-teenagers the opportunity to reach billions of people at the click of a button. And since people like to reach out to other people, that is exactly what they do. Depending on the quality of their content, this can be a blessing or a curse.

If we keep track of the number of mails we delete, unread, everyday, we'll have some idea of the scale of the content deluge syndrome.

Just as a student's inability to learn is a failure on the part of the teacher, marketers' inability to grab attention is indicative of the quality—or lack of it—of marketing messages, not a symptom of ADHD in the audience.

To suggest that human beings' intellectual capacities have declined is to perpetrate a mischievous and immensely profitable illusion—the sales of ADHD medication have skyrocketed to well over $10 billion in just a few years.

21 ILLUSIONS ABOUT WORK-LIFE BALANCE

When Pablo fell in love with Maria, her family objected to the relationship, as they felt he was socially inferior. So the two eloped, and shortly afterwards, she bore him two beautiful children, Sebastián and Manuela.

When he got home from work, there was nothing he liked more than to spend time with his family. His work was dangerous and his family feared for his safety. They loved him as much he loved them, and they stood by him, no matter what.

To anyone who saw him with his family, sharing their meals together after a prayer, it would seem like his work and his life were in perfect balance.

And yet, there was a discordant note in the story. Pablo Emilio Escobar Gaviria was the most feared man in South America. His work was not just dangerous but illegal. He was the King of Cocaine, with a personal fortune of over $50 billion. His daily work involved shipping tons of cocaine into the U.S.—and slaughtering anyone who stood in his way.

Clearly, there is more to achieving the modern ideal of work-life balance than mere walking the tightrope of balancing the time we spend on our 'work' and our 'life'.

THE WORK-LIFE BALANCE MYTH

Of course, Pablo's story is an extreme example of 'work-life balance'.

The point is that work-life balance is a myth because it is based on the flawed and dangerous premise that our work and our life are necessarily out of balance, and require some manual effort for equilibrium to be restored.

It has the insidious implication that we can do any meaningless, stress-laden, or nonsensical type of 'work', but by filling up our 'life', we can magically attain a zen-like state of balance.

The reality is that work and life are inseparable.

In fact, there is no such thing as work.

Isn't our work just *a part of our life*?

Considering that the prime time of our days and the best years of our lives are spent at work, work *is* life—and *that* is the real issue. We spend our prime time and best years working, not living. The main reason for this skewed existence is that we live peripherally, not centrally.

What is the difference between living peripherally and centrally?

To live centrally is to live from the core of our beings.

To uphold our beliefs and to live them out in every moment of our existence.

To stay true to our values, no matter what sacrifices they demand.

Living centrally is to find fulfillment and meaning in

what we do.

Few of us actually live centrally. Most of our existence is peripheral—on the edge of our real potential.

Being only a fraction of what we can be.

Doing only a fraction of what we can do.

Living life not the way we believe in the core of our hearts, but the way circumstances demand.

Or worse, living the way everybody else does.

There is nothing wrong in living the way everybody else does *per se*. The problem is that continually bowing at the altar of conformity makes us forget who we really are inside. Throughout school, college, and work-places, what is encouraged, promoted, and rewarded is conformity, whereas what we carry in our souls is individuality.

Conformity is the diametric opposite of individuality and that is *the true cause of the work-life balance conflict.*

By subscribing to the illusion of work-life balance, we perpetuate a schism in the mind of posterity. The solution cannot be obtained by merely adjusting our schedules but by adjusting our value systems.

It needs a reevaluation of our fundamental goals.

Because many of our main goals are the product of illusions, it basically involves understanding and transcending all the myths that various forms of messaging make us believe.

If we can do that, there really is no need for anyone to bother about work-life balance because our life and our work will balance themselves.

22 ILLUSIONS ABOUT CULTURE

The law of the jungle is well known, and no one enforces it better than the lion.

When a lion has a mate, his right to be with her is not permanent. He needs to reinforce his authority every now and then to prevent being dethroned. The biggest challenge faced by aging lions is from young upstarts who wander into their territory.

A clash between the reigning lion and the challenger results in one of them being banished from the area—if they survive.

If the existing rulers wins, the *status quo* prevails, but if the newcomer wins, his first priority is to wipe out the bloodline of his predecessor. He does this by brutally eliminating the rivals cubs, systematically and without mercy.

Sometimes the lionesses flee with their cubs to protect them. Not many succeed.

This macabre practice is supposedly unique to lions but is not uncommon among humans—literally and metaphorically.

ESCAPE YOUR ILLUSIONS

We have been doing it for millennia by summarily wiping out 'other' cultures and languages around the world.

MINDING ONE'S LANGUAGE

Thousands of ancient American, Asian, African, and Australian languages have been suppressed over the ages by invading cultures.

Very few have survived.

Europe, the main perpetrator of this suppression, however, has not been immune to its effects, and many European languages too are on the verge of extinction.

Today the overt invasions have stopped to some extent, but the suppression continues, though it is subtler, to the point of seeming almost voluntary.

For instance, the lesson that developing countries in Asia, South America, and Africa are learning is that the price of progress is the sacrifice of one's language and culture. These countries find that learning languages such as English is the fastest—if not the only—way for their citizens to earn more money.

Ideologies have been replaced by economics.

The current undermining of the original culture and language is primarily driven by a single purpose—to sell cheaply manufactured, globally distributed, seductively packaged, outrageously priced, commoditized products.

In a crushing irony, the actual perpetrators—the foot soldiers—of this myth on the local people are not evil, hegemonistic, global marketers but their own local peers.

For instance, more than a few schools in India

unofficially look down upon the usage of Hindi, the country's official language, by their students. The use of regional languages—the so-called 'mother tongues'—is considered low class. In one instance, linguistic prejudices in one of the country's foremost educational institutions led to the abrupt end of the a bright young girl's life.

Tired of being taunted for her 'regional accent', she committed suicide.

In the case of South American countries such as Brazil, this is a double whammy. Not only has their original culture been all but wiped out by the Portuguese and Spaniards, they now need to add English *on top of their already alien culture.*

This eradication of culture extends beyond languages.

It is evident in beautiful—and appropriate—architectural styles being replaced by unimaginative, match-box styles of modern construction.

Healthy and cheap local recipes developed over several thousands of years are replaced by the ubiquitous corn flakes—whether GMO or not— in what may only be termed a multi-level illusion, for not only is it considered more sophisticated, but it fuels the illusion of saving time as well.

In music, intricate traditional rhythms, thoughtful poetry, and complex scales are replaced by boring, repetitive beats and copycat lyrics. The results can be bizarre—such as Japanese heavy metal and Punjabi rap. Perhaps this herd mentality is best illustrated by the fact that thousands of the most popular songs of the last few decades are created using the same progressions, using the same three chords.

Barring the exceptional cases when an invading culture actually may have helped the locals—as in the case of cannibalistic societies or believers in human sacrifice or the burning of widows, for instance—such influxes overwhelmingly have been a losing proposition for those at the receiving end.

The problem, however, is not the fusion of cultures, which can be a wonderful thing in itself—an integral part of human evolution.

It is not even the loss of traditional cultures.

It is the loss of self-esteem of the 'natives' due to the illusion of superiority of a foreign culture.

It is the push marketing of false assumptions that a particular kind of music, musical instrument, culture, clothing, or diet is *cool*, while others are not.

Within the context of today's digital communications, all of this happens only to increase the sales of the manufacturers of 'cultural products' under the guise of modernization and advancement.

These marketing messages feed upon the inner need of all humans to be appreciated and to achieve, to question authority and to find self expression, which are hijacked to fuel the sale of mass-produced brands, cheap wares, and a phony culture.

The saddest part of the story is that many local people actually believe in the illusion themselves and, in the process, set themselves up for an uphill struggle in life, without ever recognizing the worth of their own cultures, traditions, clothing, language, food, music, or even their own existence.

Language and culture—traditions, festivals, music, arts, and architecture—are the stuff that make up a civilization. The product of thousands of generations, language and culture are what define us, and what we ought to take pride in.

Sadly, for many cultures around the world, it is the opposite.

23 WHY ESCAPE YOUR ILLUSIONS?

People as individuals, organizations, and communities are born for greatness; it is our destiny. The only worthy role of communication is to help as many as possible to achieve this goal by uncovering meaning and finding a purpose. The creation of wealth is one of the perks of life's journey and not its ultimate goal.

The economy exists to make people's lives better and *not the other way around.*

The economies of scale in production today consider only the financial aspect of market forces. When viewed through the wider lens of cultural, psychological, environmental, and social costs, it is often far from economical and, beyond a point, impossible to scale.

The adoption of a purely financial approach results in, *and cannot survive without*, the propagation of illusions to sustain a fundamentally faulty theory. *Maya* begins to set in before our pre-teens and rather than developing wholesome, integrated personalities, we end up with a society at odds with itself.

We have to deal with multiple personas—who *people think* we are, who *we think* we are, and who *we really* are.

Then, the interactions between people is reduced to a process of cutting through the conscious and unconscious smoke screens created by these personas, instead of a free, uninhibited, and symbiotic sharing of life experiences.

The main obstacle that we face is the lack of refinement and sensitivity of our consciousness, that leads us to navigate our lives on this planet, much like driving a truck in a china shop. Overcoming this requires achieving a 'critical mass' of awareness amongst individuals and business entities.

Several organizations have come forward to embrace new ways of thinking. Known by different names, they all revolve around the concept of a 'circular economy' as a viable business proposition, rather than a token corporate sustainability initiative. [45]

To ensure that the entire planet embraces sustainable living only requires us to ask one question: what is the future we want to create for our children and grand-children?

Maybe, a future where *everyone* would have plenty of time to be with their friends and families, sip their favorite drinks, make music and art, and go on long holidays, while working passionately on things they love, driven by their own inner desire to excel rather than the suffocating envy of neighbors or the paralyzing fear of bankruptcy.

Maybe, manufacturing will go the open source software way and companies will collaborate instead of competing.

Maybe, production will boil down to 3D printing of everything based on freely downloadable 'product recipes'.

Maybe, companies will stick to self-imposed

environmental sustainability limits on the amount of products they manufacture and the waste they generate.

Maybe, empowered citizens will co-design and co-create products side by side with manufacturers.

Maybe, war will not be the primary motive behind scientific research.

Maybe, communicators will stop creating and spreading illusions to sell stuff.

These are all maybes.

What is for sure is that, in the time that you spent reading this book, five tiny islands on this planet sank without a trace.

Maybe, hopefully, many more of us will escape our illusions before our island's turn comes up.

BIBLIOGRAPHY

1. **Castaneda, Carlos.** *The Journey to Ixtlan* . New York : Simon & Schuster, 1972.

2. **Leech, Eric.** *20 Gut-Wrenching Statistics About the Destruction of the Planet and those Living Upon It.* [Online] Tree Hugger, April 28, 2009. [Cited: September 12, 2016.] http://www.treehugger.com/clean-technology/20-gut-wrenching-statistics-about-the-destruction-of-the-planet-and-those-living-upon-it.html.

3. **Sachs, Jonah.** *Winning the Story Wars.* Cambridge, MA : Harvard Business Review Press, 2012.

4. **McGovern, Patrick E., et al.** *Fermented beverages of pre- and proto-historic China.* s.l. : Proceedings of the National Academy of Sciences of the United States of America, 2004.

5. **NCADD.** *2.5 Million Alcohol-Related Deaths Worldwide-Annually.* [Online] National Council on Alcoholism and Drug Dependence, Inc., April 16, 2011. [Cited: September 12, 2016.] https://www.ncadd.org/blogs/in-the-news/2-5-million-alcohol-related-deaths-worldwide-annually.

6. **NCADD.** *Alcohol-Related Deaths Highest In 35 Years.* [Online] National Council on Alcoholism and Drug Dependence, Inc., December 26, 2015. [Cited: September

12, 2016.] https://www.ncadd.org/blogs/in-the-news/alcohol-related-deaths-highest-in-35-years.

7. **Weissenborn, Ruth and Nutt, David J.** *Popular intoxicants: what lessons can be learned from the last 40 years of alcohol and cannabis regulation?* s.l. : Journal of Psychopharmacology (SAGE Journals). Vol 26 (2) pp. 213–220. http://dx.doi.org/10.1177%2F0269881111414751, 2011.

8. **Mark J. Pletcher, MD, MPH, et al.** *Association Between Marijuana Exposure and Pulmonary Function Over 20 Years.* s.l. : Journal of the American Medical Association (JAMA). 2012;307(2):173-181. doi:10.1001/jama.2011.1961, 2012.

9. **Asch, Solomon E.** *Studies of independence and conformity: I. A minority of one against a unanimous majority.* s.l. : American Psychological Association (Database: PsycARTICLES). Psychological Monographs: General and Applied, Vol 70(9), 1956, 1-70. http://dx.doi.org/10.1037/h0093718.

10. **Berne, Eric.** *What Do You Say After You Say Hello? The Psychology of Human Destiny.* s.l. : Grove Press, 1972.

11. **Stanford University.** *Price Tag Can Change The Way People Experience Wine, Study Shows.* [Online] ScienceDaily, January 31, 2008. [Cited: September 12, 2016.] www.sciencedaily.com/releases/2008/01/080126101053.htm.

12. **Golding, William.** *Lord of the Flies.* New York : Capricorn Books, 1959.

13. **Jung, Carl Gustav.** *The Archetypes and The Collective Unconscious (Collected Works of C.G. Jung Vol.9 Part 1).* s.l. : Princeton University Press, 1981.

14. **Carr, Allen.** *Easy Way to Stop Smoking.* s.l. : Arcturus Publishing, 1985.

15. **Choi, Charles Q.** *Quantum Record! 3,000 Atoms Entangled in Bizarre State.* [Online] Live Science, March 27, 2015. [Cited: September 12, 2016.] http://www.livescience.com/50280-record-3000-atoms-

entangled.html.

16. **Sadhguru, Jaggi Vasudev.** *Bhava Spandana Program.* [Online] Isha Yoga Foundation. [Cited: September 12, 2016.] http://www.ishayoga.org/advanced-programs/bhava-spandana.

17. **Trout, Jack.** *In Search of the Obvious: The Antidote for Today's Marketing Mess.* New Jersey : John Wiley & Sons, 2008.

18. **Falk, Dan.** *A Debate Over the Physics of Time.* [Online] Quanta Magazine, July 19, 2016. [Cited: October 2, 2016.] https://www.quantamagazine.org/20160719-time-and-cosmology/.

19. **Vegitarismus.** *Vegetarian Lioness: Little Tyke.* [Online] Swissveg. [Cited: October 2, 2016.] http://www.vegetarismus.com/vegepet/tyke.htm.

20. **Newell, Anthony Wayne and Lawrence.** The Hidden Hazards of Microwave Cooking. *Health Science.* [Online] [Cited: April 16, 2017.] https://www.health-science.com/microwave_hazards.html.

21. **Spear, Stefanie.** *House Passes DARK Act, Banning States From Requiring GMO Labels on Food.* [Online] EcoWatch, July 24, 2015. [Cited: October 2, 2016.] http://www.ecowatch.com/house-passes-dark-act-banning-states-from-requiring-gmo-labels-on-food-1882075093.html.

22. **Greenberg, Jonathan.** *Obama Expands Monsanto Doctrine By Signing DARK Act And Invalidating Vermont GMO Labeling Law.* [Online] The Huffington Post, August 9, 2016. [Cited: October 15, 2016.] http://www.huffingtonpost.com/entry/obama-signs-dark-act-to-invalidate-vermonts-landmark_us_57a644c7e4b0ccb023727b2d.

23. **Paul, Katherine and Cummins, Ronnie.** *GMOs Are Killing the Bees, Butterflies, Birds and . . . ?* [Online] Organic Consumers Association, February 14, 2014. [Cited: October 15, 2016.] https://www.organicconsumers.org/essays/gmos-are-

killing-bees-butterflies-birds-and.

24. **Greenpeace.** *Ocean plastic pollution and how you can help.* [Online] Greenpeace International. [Cited: October 15, 2016.] http://www.greenpeace.org/international/en/news/featur es/trashing-our-oceans/.

25. **Greenpeace.** *Where does e-waste end up?* [Online] Greenpeace International, February 24, 2009. [Cited: October 15, 2016.] http://www.greenpeace.org/international/en/campaigns/ detox/electronics/the-e-waste-problem/where-does-e-waste-end-up/.

26. **Larsen, Anna W, et al.** *Diesel consumption in waste collection and transport and its environmental significance.* s.l. : Research Gate , 2009. DOI: 10.1177/0734242X08097636.

27. **NASA.** *The consequences of climate change.* [Online] National Aeronautics and Space Administration. [Cited: October 15, 2016.] http://climate.nasa.gov/effects/.

28. **Berrens.** *A degree by degree explanation of what will happen when the earth warms.* [Online] Global Warming, our future. [Cited: October 15, 2016.] http://globalwarming.berrens.nl/globalwarming.htm.

29. **Berners-Lee, Mike and Clark, Duncan.** *What's the carbon footprint of ... a new car?* [Online] The Guardian, September 23, 2010. [Cited: October 24, 2016.] http://www.theguardian.com/environment/green-living-blog/2010/sep/23/carbon-footprint-new-car.

30. **Nuwer, Rachel.** *What would happen if the world suddenly went vegetarian?* [Online] BBC, September 27, 2016. [Cited: October 24, 2016.] http://www.bbc.com/future/story/20160926-what-would-happen-if-the-world-suddenly-went-vegetarian.

31. **Davis, Dr Devra.** *The truth about mobile phone and wireless radiation.* [Online] The University of Melbourne, December 2, 2015. [Cited: October 24, 2016.] https://www.youtube.com/watch?v=BwyDCHf5iCY.

32. **Leonard, Annie.** *How to Be More than a Mindful*

Consumer. [Online] Yes! Magazine, August 22, 2013. [Cited: October 24, 2016.] http://www.yesmagazine.org/issues/the-human-cost-of-stuff/annie-leonard-more-than-a-mindful-consumer.

33. **Pavlina, Steve.** *10 Reasons You Should Never Get a Job.* [Online] Pavlina LLC, July 21, 2006. [Cited: September 14, 2016.] http://www.stevepavlina.com/blog/2006/07/10-reasons-you-should-never-get-a-job/.

34. **Kiyosaki, Robert and Lechter, Sharon.** *Rich Dad Poor Dad.* . s.l. : Warner Books Ed, 2000.

35. **Waldinger, Robert.** *What makes a good life? Lessons from the longest study on happiness.* [Online] Harvard Study of Adult Development, November 2015. [Cited: September 14, 2016.] https://www.ted.com/talks/robert_waldinger_what_makes_a_good_life_lessons_from_the_longest_study_on_happiness.

36. **Robinson, Ken.** *Do schools kill creativity?* [Online] TED, February 2006. [Cited: September 24, 2016.] https://www.ted.com/talks/ken_robinson_says_schools_kill_ creativity.

37. **Eshleman, Adam.** *Probing Question: Can babies learn in utero?* [Online] The Pennsylvania State University, February 23, 2009. [Cited: September 24, 2016.] http://news.psu.edu/story/141254/2009/02/23/research/probing-question-can-babies-learn-utero.

38. **Sri Sri, Ravi Shankar.** *Sudarshan Kriya.* [Online] The Art of Living Foundation. [Cited: September 24, 2016.] http://www.artofliving.org/in-en/sudarshan-kriya.

39. **Sadhguru, Jaggi Vasudev.** *Inner Engineering.* [Online] Isha Yoga Foundation. [Cited: September 24, 2016.] https://www.innerengineering.com/ieo-new/.

40. **The Royal Institute of Technology.** *Feeling small: Fingers can detect nano-scale wrinkles even on a seemingly smooth surface.* [Online] Science Daily, September 16, 2013. [Cited: September 24, 2016.]

https://www.sciencedaily.com/releases/2013/09/130916
110853.htm.

41. **Judd, Deane B. and Wyszecki, Günter.** *Color in Business, Science and Industry.* . New York : Wiley Series in Pure and Applied Optics. , 1975.

42. **Editors of Publications International, Ltd.** *16 Unusual Facts About the Human Body.* [Online] HowStuffWorks.com, September 14, 2007. [Cited: September 24, 2016.]
http://health.howstuffworks.com/human-body/parts/16-unusual-facts-about-the-human-body.htm.

43. **Choi, Charles Q.** *Brute Force: Humans Can Sure Take a Punch.* [Online] Live Science, February 3, 2010. [Cited: September 24, 2016.] http://www.livescience.com/6040-brute-force-humans-punch.html.

44. **Sparkes, Matthew.** *Supercomputer models one second of human brain activity.* [Online] The Telegraph, January 13, 2014. [Cited: September 24, 2016.]
http://www.telegraph.co.uk/technology/10567942/Super
computer-models-one-second-of-human-brain-activity.html.

45. **The Ellen MacArthur Foundation.** *Circular Economy.* [Online] [Cited: September 25, 2016.]
https://www.ellenmacarthurfoundation.org/circular-economy/overview/concept.

ABOUT THE AUTHOR

Vivek Achary is passionate about using communications as a tool to transform individuals, businesses, and communities and to make this world a somewhat better place. He has worked for 22+ years on brand building and strategic communications for companies ranging from four-person startups to Fortune 100 companies, and has scripted award-winning animation and claymation films

A graduate from the Indian Institute of Technology, he has been an invited judge at international learning and technology awards for several years, evaluating hundreds of products from around the world. He is a certified Business Excellence auditor, and also an amateur photographer, musician, and artist.